BOBO

My Real Life Experience With the Supernatural and Paranormal Forces That Go Beyond Logic and Reason

John Frasca

BoBo: My Real Life Experience With the
Supernatural and Paranormal Forces That Go
Beyond Logic and Reason
Copyright © 2025 John Frasca

Produced and printed by Stillwater River Publications. All rights reserved. Written and produced in the United States of America. This book may not be reproduced or sold in any form without the expressed, written permission of the author and publisher.

Visit our website at
www.StillwaterPress.com
for more information.

First Stillwater River Publications Edition.

ISBN: 978-1-965733-97-4

1 2 3 4 5 6 7 8 9 10

Written and illustrated by John Frasca.
Published by Stillwater River Publications,
West Warwick, RI, USA.

The views and opinions expressed in this book are solely those of the author(s) and do not necessarily reflect the views and opinions of the publisher.

For Rachel and Rebecca Frasca

"Well, that was a huge waste of time!" We laughed it off and ended up playing some Mario Bros. The next night, we hung out again and reluctantly decided to give the Ouija board another try. Antoine's mother, Audry, wanted to give it a try, which was a shocker to Antoine and me. So the two of us put one hand each on what's called a planchette, which is shaped like a spade on playing cards, and there is a round glass window in the middle of it about 2" in diameter. This window displays the letters and numbers on the board from whoever or whatever wants to reveal to you. After a short time of putting my hand on the planchette, it felt very light and was almost vibrating. Audry said she felt the same thing, as it started moving in a circle around and around. It then started to move to certain letters, and after a few seconds, I realized what "it" was spelling. It was chronologically listing my siblings and eventually myself last, as I am the youngest of eight. My cousin's girlfriend and our friend Mike were in the room with us, and we were all mind-blown that this just happened. I asked, "Who are you?" I got no reply. It then listed a ten-digit number at the bottom of the board where the numbers are. This number was extremely familiar to me, and I said, "I know this number!" Then it hit me, it was my old phone number at my parents' house when I was about seven years old! Audry never knew this number, and I had forgotten about it, so this is undeniable proof of a third participant who wasn't visible but was undoubtedly there. Call it what you will—a ghost, a demon, a spirit, whatever but this was all the proof anyone would ever need to be a believer in the afterlife, or the paranormal. All I know is I personally felt the force and power that was moving the planchette along the board, spelling out things with accuracy and purpose. If one of us were to try to pull a hoax by moving the planchette around the way it did, without the cooperation of the other participant, it would be an almost impossible task. This was my first direct encounter with the paranormal while using a Ouija board, and I was all in.

After that night, I purchased my own Ouija board, and a few days later, I had my girlfriend Laurie and my nephew Rick over to use the Ouija board. The two of them were extremely skeptical, so I was looking forward to seeing the look on their faces if things got interesting. We put our hands on the planchette, and after a couple of minutes, it started to move. In my experience, it takes the right combination of people to get the best results, and the setting has to be good. These entities thrive off of scared or weak-minded people and are sort of timid around strong or confident people. I've been accused of moving the planchette myself, and I completely understand how a person would feel this way because the alternative makes no rational or logical sense. I've demonstrated how it would look if I moved it around the board myself while the other person had a hand on the planchette. It moves erratically and pivots around, creating a very sloppy movement. So, after a few minutes, it appeared that we were talking to my "Dad" because "it" referred to me as his "tiger," a nickname that my father gave to me. I asked him how my mother was, and he said she was good. My mother was in a bad car accident a couple of years before she passed away. I asked my dad if my mom could walk, and he said she could run, which shocked me and pleased me. I then asked him how he and my mother get around where he is, and he said, "paths." He said he drives a Lamborghini, too. My dad had a good sense of humor, or maybe he really did drive around in a Lamborghini. At that moment, the spade started to move around in a circle very aggressively, and the three of us thought this was very creepy and strange. The planchette then went to "no" very quickly. I had this feeling we were no longer talking to my dad.

I got this idea to see if this spirit could make the phone ring in the next room because I heard that some entities could have an effect on electronic devices. I asked whoever or whatever if they could make the phone ring, and it said "yes." I said that I'm gonna snap my fingers at the count of three to ring the phone. I counted... "one, two, three." To our astonishment, the phone rang. The three of us looked at each other with wide eyes. I then bravely got up and went over to the phone. I picked up the receiver and put it to my ear. I heard absolutely nothing—no static, no breathing, just complete silence. I hung up the phone, and my heart was pounding. A couple of weeks later, Laurie was at work and was in her office. One of her co-workers was standing in front of her desk, asking her something, and right behind her was a very large and very tall man wearing a black tuxedo, with his head tilted to the side, just staring at her.

Introduction to BoBo

I started using a Ouija board around 1988, and this is the first time I contacted BoBo. Over numerous sessions, he said that he was killed in Poland in the year 47 AD by an axe.

In all the years I communicated with him, I never knew that this entity might be more real than just folklore. I stumbled upon this on Google years later, in 2022. This totally validated his existence, plus scared the crap out of me.

Bobo
It's an unnatural creature from Polish folklore, a demon from Slavic beliefs.

What is the demon named Bobo?
Bobo is a demon that feeds off of fear and laughter. He can see your deepest fears and make them a reality. He gets stronger the more you're afraid, on top of his already powerful self. He is a shapeshifter and will trick you.

After seeing this, I felt like everything I experienced was more real now, if that makes any sense, and it inspired me to write this book. Once my mother died, I moved in with my sister Cassie, who lived near Boston. It wasn't long after I moved in that I started using the Ouija board again. I wasn't sure how my sister would react to the whole thing, after all, she was a devoted Catholic. I didn't want to be disrespectful, but my obsession with the paranormal drove me to use it. I had a good friend who didn't live far away, so I called Garett to see if he wanted to come over and check out the

Ouija board. Cassie's house was an old house, so the atmosphere was very creepy. My niece Leanne, who lived there, told me that a few months back, an old piano that was in the basement played by itself. She said she was watching TV one night and she heard a couple of keys being struck, and then it stopped. So, this added to the creepiness. It didn't take long for the planchette to start moving once we put our hands on it. It started to move in a circle very aggressively for a few minutes, and then I asked, "Are you an evil spirit?" It replied, "Yes." I asked, "What is your name?" It replied, "BoBo," and it continued spelling BoBo over and over. I asked, "Do you know that you're dead?" It replied, "Yes." I asked, "How did you die?" It replied, "Ax." I asked, "You were murdered by an axe?" It didn't reply. I asked, "When did you die?" It replied "47." I asked, "The year 47 AD?" It replied, "Yes, in Poland." I asked, "Did you know there is a piano down in the basement?" It replied, "No." I asked, "Will you go downstairs and play it?" Garett said to me, "NO, are you crazy??" It didn't reply. A few minutes went by, and I could feel my hand that was on the planchette get heavy. I asked, "Did you see it?" It replied, "I can't find the goddamn thing." Which I thought was strange because I figured, as a spirit, you could see everything, and I also found it strange that it didn't take credit for the piano playing. I asked facetiously, "Are you blind?" It replied, "Yes". I wasn't sure if that was a serious statement or an attempt at humor.

So, I asked, "If you found the piano, could you play it?" It replied, "Yes."

Garett and I were just staring at each other with nervous anticipation, waiting for this old, decrepit, out-of-tune piano to start playing by, for all intents and purposes, a demon. I had checked out this piano shortly after I moved in, and between the piano and the creepy vibes I got from being down there, this just accentuated the frightening feeling I already had. You could've easily used this basement as is to film a scene for a horror movie. After about three minutes or so, we heard nothing, which was a relief. I'm pretty sure I would have fainted or something if that piano started playing downstairs, in the basement, in the dark, upon request by a ghost. I don't know why I was compelled to do so, but I started to insult this spirit by saying he was weak and pathetic. Maybe it was nervous energy, but the planchette started going in a circular pattern very aggressively, and it pulled away from me. Garett was totally spooked. I asked, "Where are you in the room?" The planchette then turned on its axis to around "9 o'clock," where it was just total blackness. We had only a small candle burning in this huge dining room with high ceilings. There must not have been a moon out that night because, as much as I tried to see over where he said he was, I saw nothing. Garett was sitting directly in front of me, and he couldn't see anything either. BoBo then spelled out "don't look behind you." Garett immediately said to me, "John, please don't!" I couldn't resist the temptation, so I looked behind me. I didn't see anything, but I can only imagine what was there unbeknownst to me. The air felt heavy; I can tell you that. I turned around, and as soon as we put our hands back on the board, the planchette was slapped away from our hands with great force across the room. We called it a night after that because our nerves were shot. I didn't fall asleep until early morning that night. A couple of weeks after that night, my brother-in-law Dan found a three-headed serpent humanoid porcelain figurine inside one of the gutters on the house. I unfortunately didn't see it because my sister threw it away, but she told me all about it. I told her I wouldn't use the Ouija board at her house anymore to put her mind at ease.

However, I would certainly continue using it because things were getting very interesting.

I was getting a reputation among certain family members and friends, as if I were some sort of warlock. My girlfriend Laurie told her friends about all the crazy paranormal stuff that was going on. So Laurie and I went to one of her friends' places to show them the board. Her friend Heidi and her boyfriend Frank were a little nervous about the whole thing. We had a few drinks and chatted for a bit. It's funny because when I was talking to Frank, one of our topics was about movies. I was telling Frank about the movie "Cobra" with Sylvester Stallone, and as soon as I said all that, the TV said, "We're not going to show our regularly scheduled programming, but instead we'll bring you Cobra, starring Sylvester Stallone." We looked at each other, and Frank said, "No way!" I was like "What??" That was too weird, we thought. So that pretty much set the mood, we shut off the lights and lit a candle. We each put one hand on the planchette, and I asked, "Is there a spirit in this room?" The planchette started going in a circular pattern, and it was very strong. I asked, "BoBo, is this you?" It didn't answer. It just kept going around and around. I've noticed that the spirit world can be unpredictable, and some spirits don't like complying with commands or questions. In fact, they like to wreak havoc when you least expect it. Anyone who uses a Ouija board has no idea who they're talking to. For all you know, you're trying to communicate with an extremely ancient soul from ages ago, and their language is unknown to anyone. You may be trying to communicate with a strange demonic creature from another world whose energy just happened to cross paths with you at that exact moment. The beautiful thing about this is that it cannot be debunked, nor proven. In other realms, I believe that anything that can be imagined can exist. I mean, if the "Boltzmann brain" theory exists, then why not mine? So, this spirit apparently didn't like the typical Q&A kind of session. I noticed a mirror on the wall next to me, and I figured I'd get creative. I asked the spirit, "Do you see the mirror next to me?" It replied, "Yes." I asked, "If I look into it, can you show me what you look like using my eyes?" It replied, "Yes." Laurie, Heidi, and Frank all looked at me like I was nuts. So I got up, walked over to the mirror, and looked into it. I don't know if my mind was playing tricks on me or what, but I swear it wasn't me I was looking at. My face looked bigger with larger eyes, a bigger mouth, and bushier eyebrows. I looked at "myself" for about five seconds and no longer because I felt like I was going to get possessed or he was going to jump through the mirror, or I don't know what. I didn't want to see something that was going to traumatize me for the rest of my life, so I moved away from the mirror. I went back into the kitchen to join the others and described to them what I saw. They were all freaked out, as you would expect, and I have then slowly but forcefully went to yes. I asked, "Can you see her right now?"

He replied, "Yes." I asked, "What color car is she driving?" He replied, "Green." I thought this was strange because her car was a dark maroon color. I asked, "When she gets here, are you gonna act the same way?" Before I could finish asking this question, the planchette moved to yes on the board so incredibly fast that it made the three of us jump back a bit, and we took our hands off immediately. The speed at which the planchette moved was utterly ridiculous and downright freaky. It just seemed to almost teleport from one spot on the board to another. It moved about ten inches on the board, at what seemed to be an incalculable speed. That's why we jumped back because it was like a small explosion of energy. At that point, we decided to take a break. I convinced Rick and Antoine to put their hands on the planchette for just one more question. The energy was strong, so I wanted to take advantage of it in any way I could. It was a little after midnight, so I asked, "BoBo, we're gonna take a little break and we'll be back at 1:00, okay?" He replied, "Yes." The three of us went to the kitchen, which was the next room over. We grabbed a bite, had a couple of beers, and talked about guy stuff—sports, women, whatever. Not too long after we went into the kitchen, we heard a loud bang coming from the room we had just been in. We rushed there to see what was going on, and I noticed that my large history book had fallen off my drawing table. It was one of those adjustable tables to change the angle, and I had it set at about ten degrees, basically almost flat. I had the book in the upper corner; it wasn't hanging off or anything, and the book was on the floor directly below that corner. You would think that the book would have slid down or something, but that wasn't the case; it was very strange. My nephew Rick noticed the time on the clock on the wall. It was 1:00, and BoBo was reminding us to play. The three of us looked at each other with horror mixed with excitement. I wanted to try an experiment, I wanted to see if BoBo could move the board itself, instead of using the planchette. We each put one hand on the board, and we stacked our other hands off to the side. I asked BoBo, "Can you move the board?" Amazingly, the board slowly started to move, and it picked up speed. It was now moving back and forth with great force. I asked Antoine and Rick if they thought BoBo could lift the board off the floor. Rick was freaked out and was against the idea. I told him that this is a once-in-a-lifetime kind of thing and that we should give it a shot. Of course, part of my idea was to blow the candle out, so there would be total darkness in the room. Rick agreed, so we blew out the candle, and now it's completely dark, and I couldn't see one foot in front of me. I asked BoBo, "Lift the board off the floor." The board started to move back and forth as it did before, only with greater intensity. After a few minutes of this, I said,

"Are you unable to lift it?" The board moved back and forth with even greater intensity now. I started yelling and swearing, calling him pathetic and weak. The board then lifted off the floor about two feet. I couldn't believe it happened. I was terrified and excited at the same time. Through the darkness, Rick and Antoine shared my sentiments. When the board was at its highest point, I slightly pushed down on the board because I wanted to see how much force was being applied, and it was as if the board was on top of a table and felt immovable. My hand was on top of the stack on the side, and I briefly ran my hand under the board, and there was nothing but air. This was another valid example of the paranormal being a real thing. After about two minutes of the board being levitated, it slowly drifted back down to the floor. We put our hands back on the planchette, and it was barely moving, so I figured BoBo, whomever or whatever, didn't have enough energy to continue. But what had just happened was beyond surreal, beyond logical comprehension, and certainly the laws of physics, reason, or logic. As spooked as I was by all this, I was equally fascinated and needed more. As for Rick and Antoine, that would be the last time they would use a Ouija board.

Now it's 1990, and I made a new friend while working at a department store in Swampscott called Bradlees. His name was Derek, and he was quite a sight to behold. He was 6'10" tall and had this deep, menacing voice, but

I thought he was a good kid. After a few weeks of working together, Derek started coming to the gym with me. Back then, I worked out seven days a week, a little excessive, I know, but it took my mind off my depression in my life, plus I had plans on being a bodybuilder. I guess Derek was a bit of a drinker and dabbled with drugs, according to his parents. I was hanging out over there a couple of times a week, so his parents told me this. They were so appreciative of the fact that their son was working out and doing something positive with his life that they invited me to join them to go to Germany, France, Amsterdam, and Belgium. I got acquainted with Derek's family quite a bit. His father was an interesting character, and I guess he was from Germany originally. Derek's grandfather was a Nazi during WW2 on a submarine, and Derek's father showed me all the memorabilia he had in his study. He showed me one of the albums that the Germans would play at the concentration camps. He also showed me a .22 Luger pistol that his father would holster during the war. Then he pulls out this small book that says *Mein Kampf* on it. I had never heard of it back then, but Derek's father got me up to speed on the gist of its contents. He had some interesting things to say about what he thought of the holocaust, and that's all I'm going to say about that. I started reconsidering my European trip with them, but selfishly, I bit my tongue, because it's not every day you get a chance to go to Europe, all expenses paid! We

many people are in this room?" He replied, "Three," which was the correct answer. I asked BoBo, "Do you know who Derek is?" He replied, "Yes."

So Tonya and I were facing each other, and Derek was on my right. I asked BoBo, "I want you to point to where Derek is." I asked BoBo to do this because I knew it would scare the crap out of Derek, so after about twenty seconds, the planchette started to slowly and heavily turn because you could hear the creaking from the downward force. It took about thirty seconds for the planchette to turn around and line up to where Derek was standing, and then the creaking noise stopped. I looked at Derek, and he was pretty much wigged out, same for Tonya. I asked Derek, "You wanna try the mind-reading thing now?" I could tell Derek was scared, but he tried to downplay it and replied, "Yeah, let's do it, but I know it isn't going to work." I said, "Maybe you're right, we'll see." I told Derek to write a number on a small piece of paper, no more than three digits, and not to let anybody see it. I told him to put the piece of paper in the bathroom sink in the next room. Derek tried to be slick and wrote down 999, suggesting the obvious pick would be 666, but instead, he flipped the number. I asked BoBo, "Did you see the number that Derek wrote down on the piece of paper?" BoBo replied, "Yes." I said, "Tell us what the number is." He replied, "999." Derek immediately ran out of the house, and I followed him. He started to light a cigarette, and he was visibly shaking as his hands were trembling badly. He told me that when he was a little kid, his father punished him by locking him in his room all day. He said he didn't want to do his homework, so he crumpled it up and threw the paper under the bed. He said right after that, a new, uncrumpled sheet of paper came flying out from under the bed. He said he went to the other side of his room, just staring at the darkness under the bed, expecting something else to come flying out, or who knows what. He told me he would hear whispers in his room at night, from under the bed or from the closet. He screamed at his parents to let him out and tell them what had happened. His parents didn't let him out because they thought it was his attempt to get his parents to release him from his bedroom imprisonment. As he was telling me all this, I felt kind of bad that I started this whole mess and released Derek's childhood suppressed memories, but at the same time, I was relieved that the session went as well as it did. You don't always get good results when trying to contact the spirit world. I guess I was so determined to prove Derek wrong and to throw a scare into him that I didn't stop to think about any repercussions. Of course, I didn't know about his experience, while being locked in his room, etc. I was very grateful for the opportunity to go to Europe on their dime, and for the most part, I had a great time. I didn't try to communicate with any paranormal entities while over there, but it would have been interesting to see what would've happened if I had.

About six months have passed since using the Ouija board. I had just graduated from The Art Institute of Boston, and my life was on the busy side, trying to pursue a career as an illustrator. Being a young guy, my social life was busy as well. It was the summer of 1991, and my cousin Antoine and I were at Hampton Beach in Hampton, New Hampshire, playing some volleyball on the thick white sand, soaking up the sunshine. I've been to Hampton Beach plenty of times since, but I believe this was my first time up there. As I was playing, I noticed a handful of beautiful women, and I could tell that a couple of them showed an interest in me. One of them even gave me a smile, so it wasn't long until I went over there to chit-chat. Antoine and I introduced ourselves to the women, and I started talking to the one who smiled at me. Her name was Jackie, and we hit it off rather quickly, so much so that I moved in with her about two months later. My head was basically up my ass back then, so I figured, "Why not?" Shortly after I moved in with Jackie, I decided to have my friend Garett over to use the Ouija board, to see if we could connect with BoBo. We hadn't used the Ouija board together for about four years, so I figured things would get interesting. I picked him up at his house in Chelsea and drove back to my place in Dracut. My girlfriend wasn't keen on the idea of Garett and me using a Ouija board in her house, but I shmoozed her and she gave in. I know, I was a real jerk back then and very selfish. Believe me, treating her like that and others is one of my regrets in life. Live and learn, I guess. Jackie decided to stay with her mother's for the weekend and headed over there before I got back home with Garett. On my way home, Garett and I were catching up on a lot of things, one of which was BoBo. Garett was finishing up the candy he was eating, and it came in a little box like you'd see with 'Good and Plenty' or the like. I decided to use the little box as a planchette to see if we could communicate with BoBo on the spot. I was the equivalent of a junkie who needed a fix right away, and I couldn't even wait until I got home to use the Ouija board. I had a problem, but I didn't care at the time; I needed my paranormal fix. BoBo delivered the goods, though, because

BOBO 25

AS SOON as we put our hands on the box, it got slapped out of our hands and went flying to the back seat. We used the armrest console between the front seats as the "board," and that candy box got launched. We figured it was BoBo, but it's hard to say without letters.

In my experience, BoBo seemed to be more powerful than others, and whenever Garett and I used the Ouija board, it seemed that BoBo was the only spirit we talked to. Right before I got to my place, there was a jogger on the right shoulder, about one hundred feet away from us. Suddenly, the steering wheel starts turning towards the jogger! I'm a strong guy, and it took both my hands plus Garett's help to straighten the wheel. I couldn't stop because there was someone right behind me. Can you imagine if I had run that guy over and he died? Who would believe me that an invisible force made me kill him? I would look like one of those loonies on the news saying, "I heard voices telling me to kill him," or "the devil made me do it." We hadn't even gotten to my house yet, and things were getting crazy already. Shortly after we got there, we didn't wait long before I broke out the Ouija board. I just want to say that these incidents of paranormal activity I talk about are the best of the best of my encounters. Sometimes very little happens, and other times nothing at all. It would be a very boring book if I documented all the activity I've had, good or bad, so I don't want readers to think that every time I go near a Ouija board, the chandelier starts swinging. Like I mentioned before, you need the right combination of people, meaning no goofballs or people who don't take the paranormal world seriously and have an open mind. The setting must also be right; I wouldn't use a Ouija board on the subway, for example. If the conditions are right, I'd say every ten times I use the Ouija board, I'll get good results twice. You just never know when you're going to have a good session, it's a little like fishing in a way, you never know what's lurking about. On a few occasions, I went to the cemetery with a Ouija board and had no results. Another time, I used it at an old insane asylum turned into condos, and nothing happened. I guess the spirits aren't fans of Hollywood and don't buy into cliches. So shortly after we got to my place, I broke out the board, and we had activity right away with the planchette going back and forth very forcefully, which turned into a circular pattern. I wasn't surprised that it was working the way it was because Garett and I usually had good luck connecting beyond the veil. After about an hour or so, Garett started complaining about seeing tiny black spots all over the kitchen, where we were. He asked me if I was seeing them too, and I told him that I wasn't. I was getting a little nervous as I'm thinking, "How is he seeing these spots, and who is responsible for it?" I asked BoBo, "Why am I not seeing the same spots as Garett?" In so many words, BoBo said that I'm not susceptible to hallucinations or possession. I had an idea of arm-wrestling Garett to see what would happen because I was stronger than he was, but maybe under possession, that would change. I was more right than I knew because as soon as we locked hands, I could tell right away that the grip I was feeling did not belong to Garett. I couldn't believe the newly acquired grip he had and the force behind it. I had to pull my hand away quickly. I truly believe that if I hadn't pulled my hand away when I did, Garett was gonna break every bone in my hand. Garett then started complaining that the same arm was completely numb, and he said that it felt possessed. I was thinking, "Holy shit, what did I get myself into?" After a few minutes, luckily, the numbness in his arm subsided. Things were getting intense, and when the connection is strong, you've got to ride the wave as long as you can.

I don't know where I get these ideas, but I was wondering if BoBo would have enough strength to be able to move a pencil around and write on a piece of paper. I guess I underestimated BoBo's abilities because as soon as Garett and I held the pencil with one index finger and thumb lightly, the pencil then felt as if it weighed twenty pounds, and then began writing on the paper. I just couldn't believe my eyes that this invisible force was able to write legible words on a piece of paper in a language that we could understand. I suppose it's no different than when the planchette moves around the board and spells words out, but there's something about the pencil writing out words that makes it seem creepier and more direct. After a few minutes of writing, I realized that the person we were talking to was my mother, or someone or something pretending to be her. This entity filled an entire sheet of paper with words that were shaky but legible. The letter started off with "I miss my baby," which is what my mother used to say to me from time to time because I was her youngest. It continued saying that she was proud of me when I painted murals in my sister Cassie's house a couple of years prior. One of the things I painted for her was a Monet-style landscape with flowers and wheat fields, which came out rather nicely, if I may say so. My mother said that she watches over me, which I kind of already suspected. My mother and I had a good relationship, especially towards the end of her life. My father had died four years before she did, and for those four years, I catered to her as much as I could. In the summers, I worked construction, and I would give her most of my pay. Sometimes, I would write a phony letter like it was a bill or something, but I would put around $500 in it, and usually she would get teary-eyed, and so would I. Sometimes I could hear her in her room crying, most likely from missing my dad. So, I would go into her room and watch TV with her to keep her company. I didn't have a girlfriend either because I felt like that would have taken up too much of my time with my mother. She was in a very depressed state of mind, so my social life was nonexistent. She was in a bad car accident right after my dad passed, and she had to get hip surgery. The surgery didn't go well, I guess, because she had to use a walker for about a year afterwards. I felt like she should've been on the walker for six months or so, maximum. One day, I told her that it's time to go back to the crutches and eventually no crutches. She was apprehensive, but I told her that she just had to put in the work, and I would help her. She hated the walker, but I knew that she didn't want to part with it because she was so used to using it. I said that if she didn't make the switch right now, she'd never do it. So, I took the walker, threw it off the back porch two flights down, grabbed the crutches, and said, "Here you go." She was nervous, but she used them for about six months, then I took one away, and about six months after that, she was almost walking on her own, which was amazing. Shortly after that, she passed away, and I felt like the whole world betrayed me, even God. My soul went into a tailspin after that. After a few years of her passing, I started noticing certain things or signs that could only have been sent by my mother because the coincidences would have been off the chart. So, after this letter was "written" by my supposed mother, it gave me a feeling of warmth, even if a manipulative demon wrote it. Some of the things in the letter were only things that my mom and I shared, but BoBo was a clever one, and demons, overall, in my experience, play mind games with you and tell you things you want to hear. Garett and I were blown away by the pencil writing this letter out. It was truly beyond surreal, and it just defied all logic that a pencil being held the way we were holding it would be able to write out things. This required energy and thought, which goes against any "ideomotor effect" argument a scientist could make. The "ideomotor effect" is a psychological phenomenon where people unconsciously make tiny muscle movements influenced by expectations and desires. If Garett or I were going to try to move the pencil without the other knowing it, it would be almost impossible to write out anything, with the awkwardness of another person holding the same pencil. As a matter of fact, we tried to do just that, and it was a dismal failure. You could make the argument that the planchette moving on the board could *maybe* be linked to the "ideomotor effect" but how do you explain the 999 response to my friend Derek, without his sister or me knowing the answer, or listing my childhood home phone number that I had forgotten about and the other person using the board with me never knew? If you've never experienced what I have using a Ouija board for yourself, you could easily dismiss it as a hoax, and I would understand completely. I saw these things happen, and I have witnesses. I saw this shade-shaped object move to precise spots on the board and spell words. I saw a pencil forcefully write words on a piece of paper with very little human contact. Two other people and I saw the Ouija board itself levitate off the floor about two feet and stay there for a couple of minutes. These events go against any scientific mumbo-jumbo, the laws of physics, or anything we've been taught. They might be linked to quantum physics, something that we humans are just starting to explore, but I believe paranormal events go beyond even something as complex as quantum physics. If you try to tell anyone you had a ghostly encounter, the public will stigmatize you, so most people just keep that stuff to themselves. This letter was written, though, and my friend Garett is my witness. Most of the contents of the letter were very personal, so if it wasn't my mother who wrote it, then BoBo or whoever knows me like a book, which is frightening. We went back to the board, and I asked, "Mom, was that you who wrote this letter?" She said, "Yes." I asked, "Are you proud of me?" She replied, "Yes." I asked, "Are you in Heaven?" No reply. At that point, the planchette started to slow down a bit. I asked, "Mom, why is the planchette slowing down?" She replied, "NRG." I was fascinated by the fact that she abbreviated the word energy as "NRG." I asked her, "Are you okay?" There was about a minute pause, and then the planchette slowly went to the word "yes." There was another pause and what seemed like a loss of energy. Then the planchette started moving in a circle aggressively, and Garett and I assumed it was BoBo. I then asked, "BoBo, is this you?" We got no reply; instead, the planchette just continued going in a circle, for what seemed like ten minutes. I said to BoBo that if he didn't answer, I was going to leave the board. Then the planchette went off the board and slid off the table. Garett and I were scratching our heads as to why things were going the way they were. I then asked, "BoBo, are you here?" I got no reply. The planchette was going at a snail's pace across the board, then after a couple of minutes, it sped up a little. It spelled the name "Brandt." I asked a series of questions and figured out that this entity would be a sort of liaison between me and my parents. I asked, "Will I be able to talk to my father as well?" He said, "Yes." I suggested to Garett that we do the same thing as with my mother. So, we got the pencil and another sheet of paper, and we held the pencil the same way as we put it on the paper. I asked, "Dad, are you here?" The pencil started to move similarly to how my mother's moved, but the letters were more erratic. In life, my father had extremely neat printing, so this was weird. He wrote, "How's my tiger?" My dad always called me his tiger, so right off the bat, I felt like it was really him. Then he immediately asked me through writing, "Do you still use your radio-controlled car?" I didn't know how to answer that because right before my dad died, he got me this big gas-powered radio-controlled Corvette, but that was almost ten years prior. What he said next was like a one-two punch. He also referenced another 1983-related question. He asked me if I still played Pac-Man on my Atari. I took my hand off the pencil and got up from the table, completely perplexed. I told Garett about the car that my dad got me in 1983, and then he mentioned the Atari. Both things were from 1983, and it's as if he can't see past that point! Why didn't he ask me something about more current events, like my mother did? Instead, he mentioned two different things from the same year as his death, and almost ten years ago. The other strange thing is that my dad never knew about Pac-Man. He only knew of a different game called "Indy 500" that my brother and I were playing one time, and I asked him to play for a second. I found all this to be completely baffling on so many levels. A few years prior, when using the board at my sister Cassie's, my father had mentioned that he was in Purgatory. Back then, neither Garett nor I knew what that word meant, but that would kind of make sense if you were in the realm of a kind of punishment, but certainly not Hell, where you were able to communicate with other realms but weren't all-knowing. This is also another example of a third participant using the Ouija board with Garett and me because neither of us knew the term "Purgatory." My father's letter was shorter than my mother's, but when I compared the two, I noticed two things: 1. Each letter in its entirety had a consistent font. 2. Each letter had a different font, meaning it was indeed written by two different entities, or we're dealing with some major league deception. I found the fact that I got an invisible entity to handwrite a letter completely fascinating and had never seen anything like it. Sadly, I didn't save the letters because my girlfriend Jackie made me burn them in front of her when she returned the following day. It's a shame because the letters would have looked great in this book, but I never thought I'd ever write about this. We went back to the board, and we eventually talked to the liaison to my parents, Brandt. I asked him if I could talk to my parents tomorrow, and he replied, "Yes." So, the next morning, I compiled some questions for both my mother and father, consisting of questions like "Can you see me all the time?" and "What is Heaven like?" My girlfriend was nowhere to be found, but I presumed she was still at her mother's. I knew I'd be in the doghouse for sure from this escapade, but the reward outweighed the risk at that particular time. Things between Jackie and me were wishy-washy, so I figured, what the hell. It was about 11:00 a.m., and Garett and I decided to resume our paranormal activities. I was very eager and excited to talk with my parents about my prepared list of questions for each of them.

Like the night before, I wanted to use a pencil and paper to get my answers. I figured since it worked so well the night before, it would repeat the performance. I was wrong. When Garett and I held the pencil, a very strong and heavy force grabbed it with us and raised it about a foot off the kitchen table, then it went down to the paper. It proceeded to bear down extremely hard, making very dark lines. The pencil

then snapped in two, and I discarded the eraser end. I had a pretty good idea that whoever or whatever was doing this was not one of my parents or their liaison, but in fact, BoBo. The aggressively drawn lines were forming a Swastika smack dab in the middle of the paper, I shit you not! I'm looking out my window at my neighbor cutting his lawn as this craziness is taking place in my kitchen on a Saturday morning. He has no idea that I'm talking to some demonic entity or God knows what. It's amazing that we don't know what goes on behind closed doors. Like they say, the truth is stranger than fiction. Once the Swastika was drawn out, Garett and I looked at each other, and I remembered saying, "You gotta be shitting me!" We were still holding on to the pencil, and it started tapping on the paper, and faster and faster it went. The force behind the pencil that we were just lightly holding on to was ridiculous. The pencil tapped faster and faster, to the point where the speed was humanly impossible. I was completely fascinated by the speed of the pencil; it was insanely fast. The best way I can put it is our fingers and the pencil as a unit, moved like a sewing machine. From a physics standpoint, this movement was impossible because we weren't holding the pencil tightly. An invisible force "glued" our fingers to the pencil; even though it was a loose grip, it didn't matter, and I couldn't explain it. I've never done drugs and seldom drink alcohol, and I know what I saw, but my understanding of the way the world works almost made me distrust my own eyes. It was one of, if not *the* most amazing thing I've ever seen in my life. After about one minute of tapping, the pencil suddenly stopped. We could still feel the force on our hands, even though it wasn't moving. With me and Garett still attached, the pencil lifted off the paper. It then started heading slowly towards me, specifically my face! I said to Garett that we should probably break the connection because things just got turned up a notch. I said to Garett that on the count of three, we're gonna push away the pencil that was getting closer to me and then put the remaining piece into the trash. "Three...two...one" and we just waited to see what was going to happen. A couple of minutes went by, and it seemed that the coast was clear. I said it seemed that way, but apparently not. I didn't realize until later on that two crucifixes were taken off the wall. One in my room and one in Jackie's daughter's room. I found the one that was in my room, but I never found the one from the girls' room. Also, on the backrest of my drawing chair, were what looked like claw rips, about four of them. I thought of throwing the chair out, but I paid good money for it and taped it with black duct tape. We said a few prayers to ward away any spirits. Let me tell you that in my experience, the power of prayer totally works, and I have many examples. One of them was this guy who was a client of mine when I had a side personal training business. This guy had an NDE while overseas. I guess he drank some bad tap water and found himself on his kitchen floor. Before he knew it, he looked down at his body and was greeted by a few friendly people who told him to follow them. Suddenly, these people showed their true selves, and according to my client, they were hideous beyond words. These demons were tormenting him in complete darkness, and he heard a voice in his head, "PRAY TO GOD!" Questioning the source of the voice, he said, "I'm not religious". Again, the voice said, "PRAY TO GOD!" Once he did, the demons got more aggressive but retreated, and light poured all around him. It was God telling him that he *IS* worthy of Heaven and was sent back to fulfill his purpose. Garett and I recapped the events of the past weekend with awe and sheer terror. I decided to drive him home and then try to salvage my relationship with my girlfriend, which was undoubtedly damaged by my actions. I didn't expect much improvement on her end, after all, I turned her apartment into a paranormal magnet. Once someone invites spirits into their world, it's very difficult to close off the portal once it's opened. It's very exhausting using a Ouija board and dealing with the supernatural on so many levels. It's not a good feeling at all; I can assure you. It's the opposite of when I hit the gym and get a good pump; I feel like I can run through a brick wall. However, after using the Ouija board, you feel like your life force was sucked out of you. I think that if I had never worked out or had a "gung-ho" mentality and been introduced to the paranormal, I probably would have lost my soul to the dark forces. So, I dropped Garett off and headed home. When I got into my apartment, the phone was already ringing. I picked up the receiver, and it was Garett hysterically trying to tell me that a friend of his was also using a Ouija board at the same time as I was trying to communicate with my parents. Garett's friend asked him, "Who is Salvatore Angelo Frasca?" and Garett told him that it's my friend's deceased father. Garett's friend said that he talked to Salvatore on the board and warned John to not continue to use the Ouija board. When Garett told me this, I was completely speechless. This conversation was right out of a horror movie. Truth be told, though, I liked it. I've always been a huge fan of horror movies and the macabre in general. The warning told me that this shit is real. Not to be disrespectful to my dad or anything, but when I dropped Garett off, it was pouring out with thunder and lightning. Then, when I got home, I got this frantic horror movie phone call. How could I stop now? So, at the same time I was trying to talk with my parents, BoBo intervened violently, as a reminder of his existence and to block a warning to me. So as Garett was telling me all this, our phone call was abruptly ended. From what, I'm not sure. Like I said, it was raining out, so maybe it was a lightning strike.

    I ran into a buddy of mine, Jefferey, at the gym in the Fall of 1991, so we lifted together. During the workout, I had briefly mentioned some of my experiences with the paranormal, and he gave me a surprised look. He said, "What are you nuts?" jokingly, but then asked me, "You don't really believe in that stuff, do you?" with a more serious tone. I told him that it's kind of hard not to believe when a phone rings on command with no one at the receiving end, or a huge heavy book falls on the floor at precisely the exact time, as a reminder from a spirit wanting to communicate and lets not forget the time when my car started to steer in the direction of a jogger, requiring me and my friend to straighten the wheel to avoid vehicular homicide. Jefferey asked me if all that stuff really happened, and I said that it certainly did and lots more. I told him that I was a skeptic just like him, only a few years prior, until I witnessed many strange things with my own eyes. Jefferey's skepticism turned into intrigue, so we agreed to make time to go to his place to check out the Ouija board. A couple of weeks later, I headed over to his place with a Ouija board in tow. Once I got there, we set up shop on his kitchen island and I started asking basic questions. While trying to get a feel for what sort of spirits were hanging around, not a lot of activity took place. However, I did feel a paranormal presence lurking, and the feeling of being watched was strong. I also remember being cold and having goosebumps. It was one of those Indian summer days in late September. I didn't have an explanation for it back then, but thanks to all those ghost-hunting shows on TV, they taught me that when a spirit is nearby, they literally suck the energy out of the air. This will cause warm air to cool or electronic devices to malfunction, for instance. The spirits don't always do what you want them to do, in fact, hardly ever. They are, however, masters of the element of surprise. For example, if you ask a spirit to make a noise and nothing happens, your sense of awareness diminishes, and then you'll start talking or something. At that very moment, you'll hear a bang upstairs or a clatter of dishes. The spirits love to throw you off guard and do things when you least expect it. We started hearing cracks coming from upstairs at Jefferey's place, and they were loud. I've been in many old houses, and on occasions, you'll hear a crack or a pop from

the timbers expanding or contracting, but this was not normal. It sounded like a five-hundred-pound weight was being applied to one spot; it had that kind of force behind it. You could tell it was a heavy crack every time, and this happened about once every twenty minutes or so. Jefferey and I would look at each other after a crack and had the look of "whoa!" with it. After about one and a half hours, we walked carefully under where the noises were coming from and noticed the freakin plaster had cracked. We were reluctant to venture under that spot, fearing what on earth was making those noises would land on top of us. The real kicker of all this is that nobody lived above Jefferey, and that area up there was only a crawl space for storage. These noises were not from the house settling because they were happening left and right, and it sounded like the ceiling was going to cave in at any moment. In my honest opinion, I think it was an extremely large demon pacing the floor just to scare the crap out of Jefferey and me. Kudos to the demon because it worked. Jeffery's three-year-old son had a toy dump truck on the floor, and I had an idea. I put the truck on the kitchen island where the Ouija board was, and Jefferey and I got on either side of it. We each put an index finger on the roof of the truck. I asked, "If there's a spirit in this room, move this truck to the wall". Sure enough, the damn truck started to move toward the wall at the end of the island counter. Once it got to the end of the wall, I said to Jefferey, "Now what?"

Then, to our amazement, the truck and my hand felt very heavy, and it felt like a giant vacuum was sucking the truck with our hands on it to the wall, then the truck started to move up the wall! This was crazy because if it were just me and Jefferey trying to move this truck with just one finger each up the wall, without falling off, it would be impossible. But it did. I saw it, but my mind couldn't process it. The world is a crazy place sometimes, and there are things that we can't understand, so when we come face to face with the unexplainable, we try to tell ourselves that it didn't really happen or I must be sick or some other weak excuse to try to cope with the fact that we're adolescents on this planet. We know very little about space, the ocean, quantum physics, and lots more. Another enigmatic subject that usually gets swept under the rug is the numerous cryptids that roam amongst us, mostly in the shadows, such as the sasquatch. In my travels, I've known a few people who have seen one. Actually, two of them saw one, and the other sensed one. One guy was riding his dirtbike in Maine and stopped when he saw what could only have been a sasquatch, then the creature went the other way into the woods. Another guy saw a huge sasquatch in New Hampshire scratching his back on one of those high-tension wire towers that you see running through the forests connecting town to town with mass quantities of electricity. The creature didn't see my buddy, who was hiking, and he quietly kept it that way while backing up. The third encounter was from a girl I grew up with in my youth, whom I only chat with on Facebook now. She told me that she was jogging on a dirt road in New Hampshire with thick brush on either side of her. As she was running, she could hear heavy footsteps to her right that were mimicking her pace. When she stopped, it stopped. She said she was very fast and could run long distances, so it would be a slim chance if it were another person. Besides, she said it was a heavy bipedal whatever. So, her guess was a sasquatch, and I agreed. After talking to these people, a second or third time, the story doesn't necessarily change, but their doubts creep in because it's easier to deal with, I guess. This truck, though, no word of a lie, climbed up the wall to the cabinets. Jefferey's wife, Nadia, would've killed him if anything happened to her kitchen, and I don't think he could've blamed it on their sons' toy truck, not if he wanted to stay married.

This whole toy truck thing was another completely mysterious occurrence that simply could not be explained through logical, rational means. I mean, if you were going to try to logically and scientifically explain how a three-pound object can traverse a ninety-degree surface and move up a wall without falling with only two fingers on it, you'd be hard-pressed to come up with any sort of logical explanation. The only way you could make the metal toy truck go up that wall would be if you had about a hundred-pound magnet on the other side of the wall. I believe such a magnet could do that, but the movements would be totally different from what we experienced, not to mention you'd probably do damage to the wall from the force and friction. I decided to go back to the board again to see who was behind all this craziness. I asked BoBo, "Did you move the toy truck?" No reply, but I could sense a strong presence around. Then Jeffery's wife, Nadia, came home and thought us using the Ouija board was silly, so we stopped. Jeffery asked me if he could borrow the board to show a buddy of his, and I said, "No problem, but be careful." He then brought the Ouija board down to his car and put it in the back seat. It was now about midnight, and I decided to crash at Jeffery's place. It was late, and I didn't feel like driving home. Besides, I was a little spooked, and driving home at night made me feel a little vulnerable. About three thirty in the morning, the three of us were awoken to the sound of what sounded like ten or so full-grown men running upstairs from one end of the apartment to the other, and then it stopped. I slept on the couch; Jeffery and Nadia ran out to the living room where I was. Jeffery said, "What the hell was that?" The noise woke me up from a deep sleep, so I wasn't one hundred percent sure if it happened or if I was dreaming. I said, "You heard it too?" Jeffery and Nadia said in unison, "Oh yeah." We were all scared shitless, and I was trembling like I was cold, but I wasn't. The three of us were in total disbelief, and after about thirty minutes of no other activity, we started to get our bearings back and decided to go back to bed. I couldn't sleep after that, even though I was tired. I just lay there staring at the ceiling, expecting another calamity, but all was quiet and nothing else happened. I got up around 6 a.m. and left a note saying, "Give me a call when you're done with the board, and we'll meet up." Then I headed home. I did get a call from Jeffery, but sooner than I expected. He told me that his car wouldn't start. His car was a real land yacht; it was a late 70s Mercury Brougham, and it was a beast. The car was about eighteen feet long, and he once put a full-sized stove that he bought at Sears in the trunk and was able to close it! This car was reliable as hell; he took it everywhere, camping, tailgating at Patriots games, and even took it to the summit of Mt. Washington. He had it for about five years, and now suddenly it won't start. Not only that, but he told me that there was a strange humming sound coming from an unknown location. I told Jeffery to take it to Steve, a mechanic friend of mine, to see if he can pinpoint the problem. Steve was great; he worked on a lot of my landscaping equipment and saved my butt many a time. If anyone could figure this anomaly out, it would be him. To my disappointment, however, Steve couldn't figure out the source of the noise, and not only that, he said that he'd never heard such a noise coming from a car like this before. Incidentally, as reliable, durable, and dependable as this car was, it never started again. I felt somehow responsible for Jeffery's car dying like that, but it can't be the Ouija board's fault. It had to have been a coincidence, right?

It was the Fall of 1992, and things didn't work out between Jackie and me, so I got myself a small apartment in Salem. The number of the building was 66, and I was in apartment #6, which is crazy, right? I had a couple of strange things happen to me while I was there. The first was that, after I had been there for a few months, I had been gone for a couple of days, and on my return, my elderly neighbor asked me if I could try to be quieter at night. I told her, "Sure, no problem," but had no idea what she was talking about. Once I went in, I kinda figured it out. Most of my kitchen utensils and some pots and pans were thrown around, and my hall closet door was jammed shut. It was an old, heavy door, so it must have been slammed really hard to be stuck like it was. Another time, I was half asleep, having a scary dream of being chased by someone in the dark, and I was awoken by a woman screaming in the distance. At the same time, a huge gust of wind blew in my bedroom window, pushing in my screen and slamming my bedroom door shut. I tried not to think about these events too much because I had no other option as far as a place to live, so I just sucked it up and dealt with it. Jeffery and Nadia got themselves a new place, also in Peabody, and they invited me to come check it out shortly thereafter. It was very nice and had a lot of New England charm to it. Naturally, we talked about the events that took place the year before at their old apartment, but that didn't stop Nadia from suggesting using the board again at her new place. Personally, I didn't think that was a good idea, but my interest and needs for the paranormal prevented me from talking her out of it. We scheduled a time to meet up at their place, so a few weeks later, I went back over there with the Ouija board that allegedly killed Jeffery's car, and they invited a few other people to join in. Nadia's two friends, Julia and Marissa, and her brother Dee-Dee wanted to see the Ouija board work in person after hearing about the stuff that happened the previous year. If you've never experienced a Ouija board work properly and without the aid of any living participants, it is a truly remarkable sight to behold. Once a skeptic has determined that the planchette on the board is moving without the assistance of any visible members involved, you immediately start to rethink your reality and the world you live in. I had mixed feelings once I came to the realization that a Ouija board is anything but a game, and naturally, I was scared because it's a normal reaction to fear the unknown. Anyone who tells you that they're not or were not scared is lying. I saw this documentary once about a special forces commander over in Afghanistan fighting the Taliban, and this guy was a total badass. At one point, this guy said he went to an old underground torture chamber where ungodly acts were performed on prisoners. This chamber had a huge metal door that was completely surrounded by concrete. He was in there alone because all the soldiers were spaced apart. He said suddenly that the huge door slammed shut really hard, and there was no handle or knob to get out for obvious reasons. He immediately radioed for help, but the signal was weak because of the thick concrete walls, so it took about five minutes to be rescued. He said that he was the most scared he had been in his life; the area was abandoned for some time, and there were human and animal remains strewn about. It was so quiet, he said, waiting for his team to find him. That door was extremely heavy, and there was nobody around for miles except for his team, and they never would have closed that door on him. Whatever shut that door was very powerful and I'm sure very evil. He said that five minutes seemed like five hours. Imagine that, though, you have this total alpha male warrior who has seen some serious action and horrendous things, yet this unknown force, which in my opinion was a demonic spirit, because you can't just sneak up on these guys. They have the equipment and the training to see you coming a mile away, so he knew he was up against a force to be reckoned with. So, we were all huddled around the small, round coffee table, where we placed the board. In the living room, with one candle lit and Jeffery and Nadia sitting out, I asked my usual first question, "Is there a spirit in this room?" The planchette started to move in a circle in the middle of the board. Slow at first, then it picked up speed. It then spelled out "Julia," and we all looked at each other while Julia giggled and laughed. The few times that I've seen her, she's one of those silly people who can find humor in anything and has a very contagious laugh. I assumed it was BoBo we were talking to, and I don't think he appreciated the laughing because the planchette picked up speed and intensity. It was going in a circle very aggressively and then just stopped in front of Julia. It then turned and pointed right at her. Slowly, it moved towards her and then stopped right in front of her. I put the planchette back in the middle of the board. I asked, "BoBo, is this you?" It then slowly and heavily moved towards Julia again and again stopped right in front of her. I asked, "What is it with Julia? Do you like her or something?" The planchette once again moved towards Julia slowly, stopping right in front of her. I said that it was most likely BoBo, and Jefferey agreed with me. I said that if this is BoBo, he's never singled out anyone like this before. Nadia's brother, Dee-Dee, suggested that maybe BoBo wanted to possess Julia. We thought that was crazy, and Nadia said, "No way!" Julia was keen on the idea and thought it would be fun. Marissa tried to talk her out of it, but Julia was adamant as she giggled. We went back to the board, and I asked, "BoBo, is this you?" The planchette went over to "Yes." I said, "Is this why you kept moving to her, because you want to possess her?" The planchette again went to "Yes." I asked Jeffery and Nadia what they thought, and they said that she is twenty-two and can make up her own mind on it. Marissa thought it was a bad idea, and I agreed but kept it to myself. Dee-Dee was freaking out because he said he kept seeing dark figures outside the back windows. I asked BoBo if I count to three and snap my fingers, can you make her possessed? BoBo replied, "Yes." I said to Jeffery and the rest, "Okay, guys, get ready." One...two...three, **snap!** Julia picked her head up and looked directly at me. Her usual boisterous behavior was now nonexistent. So, I asked BoBo, "Is that you?" He looked at me and said with a deep but soft voice, "Yes." From what I knew of Julia, there's no way she could have done this with a straight face, certainly not for this long. We were all convinced this was the real thing, and I was excited and terrified at the same time. Julia's eyes were usually a very dark brown color, but now they looked very black, and her eyes themselves seemed larger. Her mouth was slightly open, as if she were deprived of oxygen. I saw total fright on everyone's faces as I looked around the room. I said to BoBo, "I want you to follow my finger with your eyes, do you understand?" He said, "Yes." I then put my finger in front of his face and began moving my finger from one side to the other. I noticed something strange; I noticed that when her eyes moved, they moved very smoothly and unnaturally. Usually, the eye moves with minute twitches to constantly readjust for light and distances, but her eyes moved as if they were ball bearings on a track or something like that. What I can tell you for sure is that it was creepy as hell to look at. My finger went back and forth a few times until I guess BoBo had had enough of my experiment and looked directly at me with a stone-cold look that sent a chill down my spine. About ten minutes had passed since I snapped my fingers, and not one giggle or chuckle from Julia, which made me think, "Where did she go?" Nadia's brother, Dee-Dee, put his hands to his face and was sobbing, unable to cope with the situation.

We were still sitting down on the sectional sofa, and I asked BoBo, "Do you want to walk?" He looked at me and said in that deep voice that clearly didn't belong to Julia,

"Yes." I then stood up and put my hand out for BoBo to hold on to. He grabbed my hand, and I helped him up. I let him go ahead of me, but I was directly behind him in case he fell or whatever, because I felt completely responsible for Julia. The kitchen was the next room over, so I asked BoBo, "Do you know where the kitchen is?" He then turned his head almost completely around to look behind me. Julia's shoulders were straight, so I had to grab her to turn her towards me; otherwise, I feared her neck would break. It seemed that if I hadn't turned Julia's body around, her head would have gone all the way around. After all, we're talking about the same demon that tried to run over someone with my own car and tried to stab me in the face with a pencil, so maybe he wanted to break Julia's neck. Once I turned BoBo around to face me, he answered my question, "Yes." Marissa was freaked out and approached the person, who was now BoBo and not her friend Julia. Marissa put her hand on BoBo's right shoulder, and then he punched Marissa square in the chest without even looking at her. Dee-Dee then ran upstairs and said, "Goodnight, I'm outta here!" I asked Marissa if she was alright. She said "yeah" in a scared voice. Jeffery and Nadia were whispering behind me. Then Nadia said, "Maybe we should stop this." BoBo turned his head to Nadia and then just stared at her for what seemed like an eternity. The silence was deafening after that, and you could hear a pin drop. I asked BoBo, "Do you want to walk into the kitchen?" Then, without turning his head, he looked at me out of the corner of his eye and said, "Yes." So, as he walked, I was on his right side, holding his arm. He walked very gingerly; it was as if he had never walked before or for a very long time. I asked BoBo, "Is Julia okay in there?" He turned his head slightly to me while walking forward and said, "Yes." Jeffery, Nadia, and Marissa followed behind me as we ventured into the kitchen. BoBo was scuffing his feet as we walked, and once we got into the kitchen, he started looking at everything. He picked up various items as if he'd never seen them before. He picked up a book of matches, a potholder, and a spoon. I asked him, "Do you know what these things are?" As I took the spoon from him, he turned his head to me and said in that deep, creepy voice, "No." I looked back at the others, noticing their fearful expressions as I was thinking, "How could he not know these objects?" Even to this day, I still don't know the answers. It's as if he crossed dimensions into ours, and those items don't exist in his. The world is a strange place, and we don't really know anything beyond our three dimensions. Some quantum physicists will tell you that there is an infinite number of dimensions, and others claim the same regarding the number of possible universes. So, our understanding of anything outside of our realm is at the early stages for sure. BoBo then went over to the wall phone, which was the norm back then, and picked up the receiver. As I mentioned earlier, we only had one candle lit in the whole house, so it was very dark. The wall phones from yesteryear had a backlit keypad to make the numbers clearly visible, and anyone who remembers those phones remembers how bright the light was. So once BoBo saw that light, it startled him. Suddenly, Julia looked back at us, chuckled, and said, "What the hell am I doing here?" Once we filled her in on what happened, she was fascinated and upset because she didn't witness any of it. She said she had no recollection of any of it, which I guess makes sense, but how crazy is the whole concept of possession? So, in fact, the human body, as a vessel, can hold more than one soul. I'm amazed at how the human body and nature as a whole works. The brain, for instance, with its ability to problem solve and with various emotions, humor, and millions of other subtle functions, not to mention the concept of consciousness. Julia also found it very funny that Dee-Dee ran upstairs because he couldn't handle it anymore. I was very happy and relieved to see Julia back to her old self again. We were meddling with unknown forces that could have caused life-altering consequences. These events with Julia were most likely the creepiest experience I've ever had, even to this day.

Some time had passed since I messed around with the Ouija board, especially after what had happened the last time. It was emotionally exhausting and spiritually taxing. We didn't think things through regarding Julia. There was no guarantee BoBo would have returned her once we were finished. I had no intentions of ever getting someone possessed; I didn't even think it was a possibility. It just happened, and I got caught up at that moment, I suppose. I can't even imagine how bad I would feel if something permanent happened to her. We were screwing with powers beyond our control and understanding, and thankfully, things turned out all right. However, years later, Julia had some issues with suicidal thoughts and strange things that happened to her regarding poltergeist activity in her home. Also, her daughter-in-law was involved in a freak car accident that took her life around 2018. I certainly doubt these occurrences were triggered by paranormal forces, but it's the first thing I thought of. Julia's older sister Diane had a lot of strange things happen to her, and some of her teenage children also. Diane had a ghost of a little girl that would haunt her frequently. She told me that on many occasions she would see this girl standing at the foot of her bed just staring at her or seeing her in the reflection of the TV screen when it was off, sitting next to her, which I found frightening. She also said that every now and then, you could hear the disembodied voice of a little girl from various spots in the house. Diane's two teen daughters, Mariah and Addison, would have pictures turned upside down, things strewn about, and just about any poltergeist activity you could think of would take place over their house. I don't know if

BoBo was responsible for these occurrences or not, because I hadn't used the Ouija board or tried to contact him for well over a year. So maybe this was him trying to get my attention. Whenever I saw Jeffery, he would fill me in on these things, and I told him that I wanted to use the board over at Diane's house because, like me, she had a strong connection with the paranormal. So, the thought of the two of us joining forces could be pretty epic. It was now the Fall of 1993; I had just purchased my first new vehicle. I said to myself that I'm going to go to the Ford dealership over the next town and get myself a nice, practical, economical, and affordable car. When I walked into the dealership, they had this shiny royal blue, small-sized, sporty pickup truck with mag tires and shiny chrome rims. It was on one of those spinning platforms, and I just had to get this truck! So, a few days later, I got it and I figured I'd take it around for a cruise. It was a gorgeous Saturday; I was cruising around, and I decided to swing into the McDonald's drive-through and get one of those vanilla milkshakes. As I was pulling up to get my shake, I noticed Dee-Dee hanging out the window. I said, "What's up, man, you work here?" Dee-Dee said, "Yeah, I'm the assistant manager." I told him how glad I was for him, as I was waiting for my shake. Dee-Dee went to hand me the shake, and right before I grabbed it from him, it was slapped very aggressively from our hands. We both looked at each other and said in unison, "BoBo!" I said to Dee-Dee that I didn't need a shake that badly, and I drove off, waving bye. It's crazy because it had been a while since I tried to communicate with any spirits, so why the strong connection? I was puzzled and could only think of one rational explanation for him being right there to intervene with me and Dee-Dee, and the thought of it terrified me. The explanation is that I think he stays with me all the time. Otherwise, how do you explain him to be right there? That shake was slapped out of our hands because it went behind us like five feet back, plus you could feel the force behind it. It wasn't just dropped either, or a case of the butterfingers. I've seen Dee-Dee a handful of times since then, and we don't talk about it because we don't have the words.

Life got more hectic for me. I was in the beginning stages of starting a landscaping business, which took up a lot of my time. Not to mention, I was in a semi-serious relationship, so my free time was at a premium. A few years had passed, and it was now 1997, and my paranormal activity was nonexistent. The only strange or unexplainable things that happened to me over the last few years was one night I was taking a shower alone in my apartment that I shared with my girlfriend, Jan. For no apparent reason, I started thinking of BoBo, while I had my shower radio blasting and POP! The power went off, and now it was eerily quiet. Jan and I were renting out this old Victorian-style apartment in Braintree, which had a lot of charm and history to it, with its ornate wood carvings, chandeliers, and a winding staircase. You know, your basic horror movie house. I shut the water off, even though I still had soap in my eyes, and I could swear I heard talking upstairs. I put my hand on the shower head so I could hear better, and I heard it again, a woman's voice. My eyes were stinging from the soap, but I was so nervous from what I just heard, it didn't matter. Now all alone in the pitch-black darkness, I put my bathrobe on and ventured upstairs. I could almost hear my heartbeat from the quiet, plus I was wigging out. I remembered I had a small flashlight in the entry table drawer at the top of the stairs. The voice was a woman's voice that was unintelligible, and it sounded like it came from the guest bedroom in the back left corner of the second floor. I got the flashlight and went to the bedroom. I panned around with the light and saw nothing. I then heard a small crashing noise back where I was at the top of the stairs near my bedroom, and I noticed that the smoke detector had come dislodged from the ceiling. I felt like someone was standing right in front of me, giving me the death glare, and my blood ran cold. As much as I wanted to stand my ground in my own house, I just went down to the kitchen to light a candle and wait for Jan to get home. Ghosts - 1, living occupants - 0.

    The other strange thing that happened not too long after the power outage incident was one evening when I was relaxing in the tub, and over by the bathroom sink, I noticed my toothbrush was moving back and forth inside the porcelain toothbrush holder on the wall. It did this four or five times and then stopped. It moved purposefully and intentionally, and it wasn't the wind. Strangely, I wasn't scared to see this, and I didn't feel that the spirit was malevolent in nature. So, I just enjoyed my bath and actually fell asleep from being so relaxed. I woke up maybe fifteen minutes later, and I noticed something peculiar. Usually, after a while, the water level in a tub goes down a little, but I realized that the water level has gone up about two inches, just below the overflow drain. I'm thinking, "This doesn't make any sense, and I know how much water I had in the bath." I know that the water wasn't as high as it was now, then I realized that could only mean one thing: I'm not the only one in this tub. So, I nervously got out with my heart pounding and my head spinning because I was so freaked out. I had told Jan all about my Ouija board experiences from years past, and she said she wanted to see it work with her own eyes at some point. I told her that I wasn't sure if I wanted to use a Ouija board again, but she convinced me. Of course, this wasn't hard to do because after a few years of not using the board, I was eager to use it again. Jan, like me, was an avid fan of horror movies, and she enjoyed being scared. So, one night, Jan and I went over to Jan's sister Karen's house to see who we could contact. Karen's husband, Paul, had just come home from work, and he just wanted to crash until he heard we brought over the Ouija board. After all the stories he had heard, he was anxious to join in. So, the four of us huddled around the board, which was on top of an old chest. Karen was somewhat of a hippie, and her place was decorated in 60s and 70s style. During the time we used the board, the planchette would erratically move around, varying in speed and level of strength, which was something I've never felt before. It almost felt like more than one spirit was trying to communicate with us, and it kept spelling "yoyo" over and over. This went on for at least twenty minutes, and I said to the others that if this continues for the next five minutes, we should just call it quits because this whole "yoyo" thing is getting ridiculous. Well, needless to say, the status quo did not change, so we ended the session.

We had high expectations, but unfortunately, the evening was uneventful. About three weeks later, Paul went to visit his mother in Sudbury. She asked Paul if he could get something from the attic. It was one of those ladders you pull down from the ceiling, so when he climbed to the top, he saw right there in front of him an old wooden yo-yo. He said he couldn't believe what he was looking at, and the whole thing felt surreal. When Paul told me about it, I was shocked and felt vindicated at the same time. They say that spirits roam in higher dimensions, and they can see the past, present, and future simultaneously. So, the yo-yo was probably inserted into Paul's reality and timeline. I didn't, however, understand the significance of the yo-yo.

It's now 1999, and for reasons I didn't know, my sister Cassie took her own life. I can only speculate on what caused her to do such a thing. Her method of suicide was jumping off the Mystic River Bridge in Boston, some two hundred feet above the Atlantic Ocean. I saw her about six months before her suicide, when my friend Paul and I helped her move out of her house and into an apartment. I noticed that she had gained a lot of weight since I saw her last, which surprised me. Cassie was always fit and usually had a physically demanding job to keep her that way. She's worked on a construction site, been a parcel delivery driver, and was even a member of the carpenter's union. I think moving out of her dream home, which she worked so hard on, and then losing everything, most likely led her to her depression and thus her suicide. I was very close to Cassie; she is the reason I enrolled in art school, and she got me my first real art set with professional brushes, paints, etc. So, for me personally, her death was a terrible loss, and I still miss her contagious laugh. After her funeral, we all went back to my niece Leann's house to meet up, grab a bite, and be with family. Once we were over there, I noticed a Ouija board on a shelf in the next room. My Nephew Joel was there along with Rick, who I knew wouldn't even dare to go near a Ouija board after what had happened a few years prior. Joel, who was only a year younger than me, was familiar with my paranormal experiences, plus I'm sure Rick filled him in on what

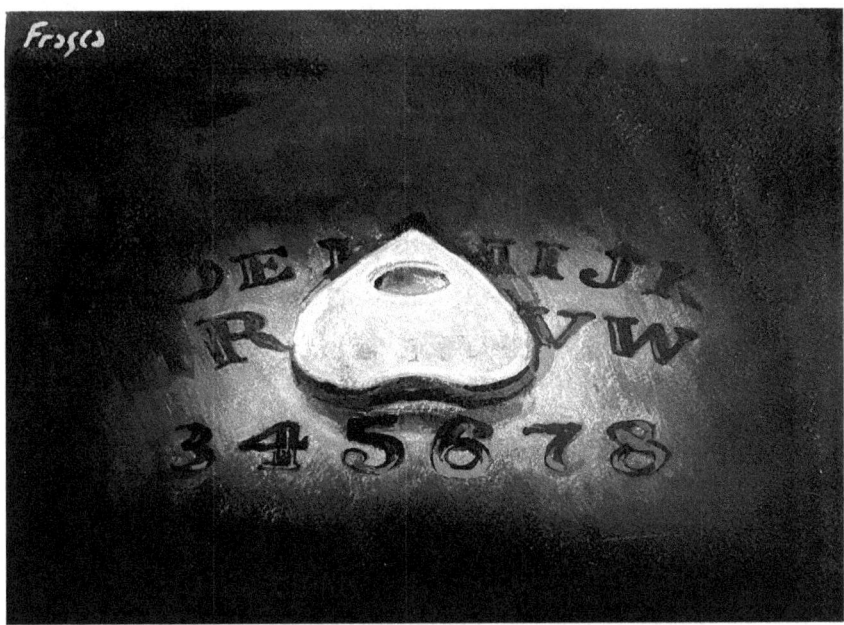

he went through before. I asked Joel if he would be willing to use the Ouija board right there and now. There was a small table off to the side in the next room that we could kind of hide behind, because I was feeling some serious vibes that are hard to put into words. I suppose it's no different than a drug addict needing their fix or a gambler putting their last dollar on a horse. I loved my sister Cassie very much, so believe me, I didn't want to be disrespectful, but I couldn't help myself. I felt drawn to the board, which sounds crazy, but I was. I got the board down from the shelf and set it up on this small card table. Rick came over to me and Joel to see what we were up to, and once he saw the Ouija board, he said, "Are you guys nuts?" I looked at Rick without saying a word and put my hand on the planchette along with Joel's. As soon as both our hands were on the planchette, SLAP!! I cannot put into words the amount of energy it took to describe the force behind the slapping away of the planchette from our hands. It was like we tried to jump a car battery with reversed polarity, only without sparks. It happened so fast that the three of us jumped back from the visual shock of it. I'm surprised the planchette didn't break off the wall when it flew from one end of the room to the other. We looked at each other with our jaws hitting the floor, and I decided to just put the board away before things got worse. I figured whoever or whatever was on the other side that just did that is way too powerful and frankly terrifying. I didn't want to be responsible for any catastrophes that might take place. Some people have said to me that maybe it was my sister being very upset with me for messing around with that sort of thing inside of her daughter's and granddaughter's house. The other theory is that it was BoBo being upset that I haven't tried to communicate with him for a while. This reminded me of the milkshake incident with Dee-Dee, how the energy level was at a ten right off the bat, suggesting that BoBo stays very close to me all the time. I went to a psychic a few months later to see what they told me. It was a woman psychic who told me that she was from a small village in El Salvador where most of the people had some sort of psychic ability. She did some ritualistic stuff with wax and water and determined that I did indeed have a benevolent entity attached to me. She said some mumbo jumbo stuff, and I gave her an item on my person that I could part with, so I gave her a key off my ring that I don't use anymore. I went back one other time and brought with me some items that she needed to ward away any bad spirits around me. I don't really know if what she did worked or helped at all, but the experience was interesting. Fast forward to 2004, I visited my brother Brett to catch up and most likely talk about the Pats, who were the best team in professional football at the time. Brett is more of a people person than I am and was very close to his neighbors. He lived in a beautiful house in a beautiful neighborhood. So, his neighbor, Maureen, decided to visit him. After a short while, I don't remember how we got on the topic, but my sister Cassie's suicide came up. Maureen showed her sympathy to me and Brett, saying that it must have been a terrible shock to lose a sibling that way. Numerous people over the years have taken their lives from that bridge by plunging into the deep, dark water. I can't imagine what was going through my sister's mind as she jumped. I can only hope she was at peace with her decision. Maureen also told us that about five years prior, she witnessed a heavyset woman jump off that same bridge. Brett and I looked at each other, and I asked Maureen, "When exactly was that?" She said that she keeps a journal, and she thought it was in 1999, sometime in February. She went next door to get her journal, and upon returning, she confirmed that the date of this woman jumping was the date my sister jumped - February 10th, 1999! Maureen said she saw a car parked in the right lane. She then saw a woman leap, as her coat filled with air. An image, she said, hasn't left her mind to this day. Think about that - to have witnessed my sister jump, which was probably a quick act going from her car to the top rail of the bridge, took around twenty seconds. So maybe five cars or so go by during this time. Out of those handful of people, what are the chances of one of those people moving in right next to my brother to share this story?? It is incalculable! That being said, you can completely rule out coincidence. So, what was the purpose of positioning Maureen on that bridge at that exact time and then right next to my brother? Just to say hello? Maybe. Or is it something deeper? To this day, I still don't know and probably will never know. I find the whole thing fascinating, though.

My landscape business was thriving, I got married and had two beautiful daughters, Rachel and Rebecca. So, life was good for me for a while, until my bad luck with women caught up with me again, so Liliana and I ended up getting a divorce in 2009. Between work and marriage, I had no time to coordinate any kind of séance, plus Liliana wouldn't have allowed it. I didn't want to bring negative energy into my home, especially with my two young daughters there. I threw away my old Ouija board before my sister Cassie's death back in 1999 and had no intentions of bringing another one into my new home. During my marriage, I did have a strange encounter back in 2005 that was completely inexplicable. Liliana's cousin Gadel was staying with us from Mexico, to take some college classes and to visit us and the girls in New England, a place she's always wanted to see. So, Liliana was upstairs, getting ready for us to go out to dinner, and Gadel would stay home to babysit. While downstairs with Gadel watching TV, we heard a huge bang from what sounded like behind the wall where the TV was. Gadel and I jumped from the noise and looked at each other with shock and disbelief. First, I checked down in the Rec room, where I was sure the noise originated from, but I saw nothing out of the ordinary. I didn't know what I was looking for, I mean, what could have made such a loud bang? The noise sounded like someone hitting the wall with the side of their fist. The sound was very human-like and blunt. So, I fully examined downstairs to no avail. I then checked outside near the front porch, thinking maybe it was one of the kids in the neighborhood playing baseball or something, and someone hit a line drive into the side of my house. I was trying to put Gadel's mind at ease and was really hoping that I would find something to explain the noise, but unfortunately, I came up short. I was reluctant to leave Gadel alone with the girls, but Liliana laughed it off, which lightened the mood, so we left for dinner. Upon returning, a couple of hours later, we found Gadel in the same chair she was in when we left. Tears were running down her face, and she was trembling. She told us she heard a deep man's voice coming from down in the Rec room. I asked her if the voice came from next door because my neighbor Bob had a deep voice. She said the voice was definitely below her, and then she heard another loud bang, only this one was louder. I was completely freaked out, but I didn't show it because it would have made things worse. I felt bad because I wanted her to have a nice time during her visit. We didn't hear any more bangs, disembodied voices, or strange things happening during the rest of her stay or for as long as I lived there, for that matter. However, from time to time, I had a strong sense I was being watched, but I don't think there was ill intent behind it. Those bangs made no sense in hindsight because nobody was down there. I believe it was from the man who lived there before us. I did a lot of renovating to the place, and I think it was him complaining about it. So, after my divorce, I was very heartbroken, mainly for my daughters having to deal with the repercussions of it all. I started going to a therapist, and he told me I should start dating. It was difficult at first because I didn't want to let go of what I had, but it didn't seem promising at all. So, I went on one of those dating sites and dated a few women. When I met Kay, we had a lot of compatibility, and she was easy to talk to. Things went well for a while, and we decided to take a little vacation. We both liked camping, so we decided to rent a cabin in either Maine or New Hampshire. Josh, one of the guys who worked for me, said that his family had a cabin up in Maine that we could use, so I accepted their offer. Josh brought his girlfriend, Samantha, so the four of us headed up there during the summer of 2012 to get some much-needed R&R. Josh was a big fan of the occult as well, so we stopped at a place on the way and I got my third Ouija board. When we got there, we had a few drinks and watched a movie. Then I broke out the Ouija board, and Josh's girlfriend did not like that idea, but the majority ruled, and we began. Josh must have been in the doghouse that night because she begged him not to use it. I hadn't used a board in about thirteen years, so I was interested to know what was going to happen. After a couple of minutes, the planchette moved in a figure eight pattern, something I hadn't seen before. It was the first time Josh and Samantha saw a Ouija board work, and they were astonished. Josh asked me if I was moving the planchette, and I replied, "Nope." Samantha was absolutely frightened, curled up on the couch with a blanket covering her entire body, exposing only her eyes. The rest of us were a few feet away at the card table with one small candle lit on the counter. It was around midnight, and it was eerily quiet outside, miles away from civilization, with no phone service whatsoever. We were upstairs in a two-floor cabin, and we kept hearing strange noises downstairs. As I mentioned, only one candle was lit, so downstairs was pitch black. The planchette continued making a figure eight pattern on the board, and for some strange reason, would go from zero to one and back on the numbers part of the board. The cabin was a little on the old side, so to turn the light on downstairs, you had to physically go down there to turn the light on. Josh assured us that the noises we were hearing were normal, but I wasn't convinced, and neither were the girls. Josh asked me if he would be able to talk to his deceased grandmother, and I told him that I wasn't sure and I didn't think that would be a good idea. I told him about the time I talked with my parents and how things didn't turn out too well. Kay said that she was feeling dizzy and just weird in general. We decided to take a break from everything, and Kay put her head down to rest. I rubbed her head and told her to relax, then she started whispering something that we couldn't decipher. She raised her head with her eyes closed and was almost frozen for about thirty seconds, but felt like it was forever. She whispered, "Josh," which startled us, as we were not expecting that. She whispered again, "Josh," then Josh and I looked at each other, puzzled and shocked. I said, "That is not Kay's voice." Josh agreed with me. The voice was weaker and elderly. I was thinking, "Where did my girlfriend go??" Josh was certain that his grandmother was possessing Kay, and I reluctantly agreed with him. Kay uttered things like "Josh, you're such a good boy" and "I watch over you." She also said, "But why did you do it?" I looked at Josh and noticed he was tearing up. I asked him, "What did she mean by that?" but I didn't get an answer. I figured it was really personal, so I let it go. She said to Josh that she put the medallion on his dresser for him to see. Josh looked at me and said that he thought it was strange that his St. Anthony medallion was out in the open like that. I just said "wow." Josh put his hands on his face and was clearly crying. I put my hand on his shoulder, and Samantha left the sofa and went to Josh's aid. Kay put her head back down for about ten minutes. When she snapped out of it, she said she was standing behind an elderly man and woman, who were looking at a young man who was in the shadows. I told her what took place over the last half hour or so, and she was astounded by it all. When Josh asked me if he thought he could speak with his grandmother, I thought, "There's no way." But the world of the paranormal is very unpredictable, and to my amazement, it actually worked. The next day, we did some fishing from Josh's boat, drank a few beers, and enjoyed the beautiful Maine weather. We were out there for about four hours and decided to head back to the cabin. It was late afternoon, and the water was getting a little choppy. We were on what's called Flagstaff Lake, and the story goes that there is an entire town submerged thirty or so feet below from a mining disaster or something like that. A beautiful day was about to be tarnished when Samantha let out a scream, claiming she saw a man and a woman dressed in outdated clothing, standing right at the shore. She said they were just standing there, facing us, and were clearly staring right at our boat. She claimed that they didn't have faces and were completely pale. I said, "What?? Where??" She pointed back and said they were about one hundred feet or so back. She said the woman was wearing a white dress and the man had black pants, a white shirt, and was wearing suspenders. Samantha said the clothing looked like 19th-century style. Neither Josh nor Kay nor I saw anything, but I wish I had because I've never actually seen a ghost. So, we circled back to where Samantha said she saw them, and there was nothing. We

were a little concerned about Samantha, figuring the shock at what happened to Kay the night before might have made her prone to hallucinations or ghostly apparitions. We stayed one more night at the cabin, and for Samantha's sake, we decided to forgo any Ouija board activity.

Besides, I think we all had our fill of creepy stuff and decided to watch some TV. We turned in for the evening around 1:00 a.m., and it was unnaturally quiet outside, void of any animal or insect noise. Kay and I just lay in bed, both agreed that something wasn't right, and the air felt heavy, like at any moment something bad was going to happen. I had this feeling that I was being watched, and my mouth was so dry. I don't think I swallowed or blinked for at least five minutes. I was going to ask Kay, "Do you hear crickets outside?" but before I could ask her, I heard what sounded like a paper cup hitting the concrete floor downstairs. I asked Kay, "Did you hear that?" She said, "Yeah." She asked me, "Can you go see what that was?" She said she would feel better and won't be able to sleep if I don't check it out. I said, "Hell no!" I didn't care that I looked like a coward for not going downstairs, especially after what Samantha claimed she saw earlier that day. Suddenly, we heard what sounded like a good-sized rock hitting the back side of the cabin. Then there was the sound of pebbles hitting the same area, one by one, around four times. I was completely frozen in fear, and Kay and I looked at each other. I couldn't figure out what could have made noises like that because we were the only ones out there for miles, and it sounded deliberate. It took me a while to fall asleep, but finally I did. I don't even remember falling asleep either; I just passed out. The next morning, we eagerly left, and I thanked Josh for letting us stay at his family's cabin. I never returned there, thankfully, or to Maine for that matter. I used to think that being in such a remote place would be exciting and relaxing, but instead, you're helpless and at the mercy of whatever or whoever is lurking out there.

The following year, I finally had the opportunity to join forces with Diane, Julia's older sister, who I mentioned before, who had a lot of hauntings and unexplainable things happen in her home. So, I thought getting together would be pretty eventful. Of all the times I used the Ouija board, or any attempt to connect with the spiritual world, I never thought to videotape it. Diane got her three teens—Mariah, Addison, and her nineteen-year-old son Nathan to join in with me and Julia. So out of the six of us, two would sit out here and there, because in my experience, four people should be the limit. So, the camera was rolling, and I pretty much ran the session. Diane's house was a quaint little house on a dead-end street, not too far from the ocean in the heart of Gloucester. We had a couple of candles lit in the pantry where we were, and the mood was creepy. BoBo had boldly suggested that we use one large red candle, and I told him that we didn't have a red candle. The last couple of times from years ago, BoBo started getting demanding, and at one point, he told me how to put a curse on people, and

I refused to do that. Strangely, though, someone who had done me wrong in the past died on a certain date and at a certain time that was very coincidental to me. In fact, I don't think it was a coincidence at all because the date and time of death were identical, matching a number significant to me. I had nothing to do with this person's death, and I didn't put a spell on them, but I think it was a message from BoBo, letting me know that he could do these things for me. I was very angry at the deceased, but I didn't want them dead! That was one of the reasons I toned down my usage of Ouija boards. So, it was very quiet, and the feeling of dread was in the air. It was the Fall of 2013, and it was beautiful outside. I asked, "Is there a spirit in this room?" Just then, some of us heard a faint crashing noise that sounded like it came from the attic. We were on the first floor, and Diane said that there was nobody upstairs. She had a cat, but it was on the first floor with us. Whatever that was, I said, was meant to get our attention. It was a very unnatural sound, and Diane agreed with me. We were way too scared to investigate, so we ignored it and continued. The planchette answered my question with "yes." I asked, "BoBo, is this you?" The planchette went over to the "B" and then the "O". He kept going back and forth, "B, O, B, O"...which was different from his usual circle pattern. It almost seemed like some other entity was copying BoBo, but who knows. After about fifteen minutes of us using the board, Nathan started complaining about his right arm going numb. He said it felt very light also, as he chuckled. As time went on, his other arm and then both his legs did the same thing by going numb. Nathan didn't seem to be afraid of this, but I was getting a little freaked out, especially since I was sitting right next to him. I asked BoBo, "Are you doing that to Nathan's legs and arms?" he replied, "No." So, either we had another spirit amongst us, which I suspected, or BoBo is being deceptive as he typically does. Nathan's arms started lifting off the arms of the chair he was sitting in, and then both his knees lifted off and rose towards him, and his feet were about a foot off the floor. There's no way he could have done that on his own because of the amount of strength required to hold that position, not to mention he wasn't even straining. Some outside force was lifting his extremities; otherwise, this was a nearly impossible feat of strength. Strangely, we didn't find this scary at all, maybe because of the silly pose Nathan was in. He said he felt light like a feather, and after about fifteen minutes, his extremities lowered slowly. He said he felt lightheaded and was a little lethargic. Mind you, I had all this on videotape, so I was pleased. I saw a pencil on the table, and I was wondering if BoBo could move it entirely on his own, without us touching it. This would be an unprecedented feat if BoBo could move an object without the aid of a living person's energy. I thought if he could move someone's limbs on his own, then why not another object? I took the board off the table and replaced it with a pencil. I was nervous and excited, and I asked, "BoBo, can you move this pencil on your own?" The six of us just stared at the pencil for about thirty seconds, and I saw it slightly move. I couldn't believe it. It moved about a half turn or about a quarter of an inch. Diane and I gave each other a high five for having witnessed that. This was a huge deal to have made this happen; for all intents and purposes, I made an invisible force move an object from my command. This was a magic trick that was a hundred percent real. To think that I have this whole thing on videotape is incredible. We didn't use magnets or any other contraptions; this was the real thing. Then I asked BoBo to move the pencil again, only

this time move it more. Again, we all stared at the pencil with excitement and anticipation. Then, amazingly, the middle of the pencil started bending upwards, and I could see light coming from underneath. Some force was pulling the middle of the pencil upwards as if it were made of rubber, but it was a regular pencil.

There ended up being a space under the pencil of about 1/8", and then it rolled about an inch, which was remarkable. One of the most amazing things about this, other than the fact that I just made a pencil move by itself, is that when the pencil moved, it moved as if someone blew it with a small gust of air. In other words, it looked very light. However, the pencil was under incredible stress to be pulled with such force as that, yet it didn't move that way. Under normal circumstances, it would take about twenty pounds of force to bend a pencil like that and to keep the ends of the pencil firmly against the table at the same time, which defies logic and certainly physics. The other baffling thing is that if you were to apply roughly twenty pounds to the middle of a pencil, it wouldn't bend; it would most likely break. Don't forget, it was bending upwards, so how would anyone be able to do that? The simple answer is, they wouldn't. I know this sounds crazy, but I'm pretty sure that whatever force bent and moved the pencil the way they did, molecularly changed the composition of it to move it that way. Otherwise, how do you explain it stretching like rubber and moving as if it's a feather? In our three-dimensional world, that pencil would have snapped in two, or if you could apply enough weight to roll it without snapping it, it would roll heavily like a stone wheel or a steel pipe, not like a feather. I recorded an impossible event, and it's a hundred percent authentic! The six of us were in total awe, and we were yelling and screaming from the excitement of having witnessed that. As we were celebrating, the pencil moved back to its original position, but we didn't notice it right away. If you look at the video, however, you can see it move back into its original position. I found this to be extremely unnerving. What happened next was off-the-charts surreal, unexplainable, and downright frightening. Most of us heard: a horse galloping! Repeat...a damn horse galloping! When you replay the tape, you can hear it as well. This makes no sense because it was only for about two seconds, it was around midnight, and we were on a dead-end street. How can anyone begin to explain that? The galloping sound was very clear, and there's no mistaking that sound. What does it mean? I have no idea, even to this day, it still baffles me. After that night, I never touched another Ouija board. I eventually got remarried and had another daughter, Kate. It's now 2025, and Oksana and I are happily married and still going strong. Oksana has two sons from her previous marriage, so there are seven of us now. My two daughters live out of state, but we all try to get together as much as possible. I realized the mistakes that I have made messing with the paranormal, and I would never jeopardize what I have by using a Ouija board again. I've learned over the years about the forces that lurk amongst us, and I've recently learned of the good in our existence, such as our Lord Jesus Christ. I'm not one of those religious nuts handing out pamphlets, nor do I go to church, but I most certainly believe in God, and he is more powerful than any dark force that exists. I pray all the time, hoping that he will save my soul for summoning demons and all the other bad things I've done, but I'm not so sure. I've learned more about relationships and how to compromise and be more humble. I'm far from perfect, but I have a great wife and kids to keep me on the straight and narrow.

This section contains strange and unexplainable events that don't necessarily fit into the chain of events described in this book. They are, however, somewhat linked, and I find them very interesting and intriguing. I hope you enjoy them.

The stone

Back in 1984, my friend Mike and I were doing what boys do: we were skipping stones at the pond. We were trying to see who could skip a stone the furthest. So, I grabbed this one stone about the size of my palm, and it was flat and disc-like. I felt I had the perfect stone to beat Mike, so when I threw it, instead of it hitting the water on its side, it made a downward turn right into the water. I was angry for wasting a good stone for nothing. Then, as God as my witness, about three seconds later, it shot straight out of the water about eight feet. I yelled to Mike, "Did you see that?" but unfortunately, Mike didn't see it. He seemed to believe me, though, as I jumped up and down describing what I saw. I just couldn't believe that actually happened. I've never done drugs, and I know what I saw. It happened so long ago; I second-guess myself, but I know it happened. My father had been gone for about a year at that point; maybe it was a sign from him. This incident was the first truly strange thing to ever happen to me.

The vacuum

During that same year, I was a junior in high school, and I was working at a toy store in Lynn. It was about thirty minutes from closing, and I was thinking of staying at my sister Judy's house, who didn't live far from where I was. I called her from a pay phone near the building. I knew that she was alone because her husband was up in New Hampshire, and I asked her if I could spend the night. This was a year after my dad passed away, so I was feeling lonely and depressed, and I needed some company. She said she didn't think that was a good idea because she just wanted to go to bed. Suddenly, I heard this strange noise in the background, and I asked her what it was. She said it was the vacuum. The only problem with that was that it was unplugged and in the closet. She started to cry in fear and asked me to stop by after work. As freaked out as I was, I needed the company more and was glad to be hanging out with my sis!

Indy 500

While I was visiting Judy, I started playing 'Space Invaders' on her Atari. I played for about two hours and hit the sack on the sleep sofa as I watched a little TV. The next morning, when I woke up, I noticed that the 'Indy 500' cartridge was in the game console. I had to really think hard about whether I used this game or not. Then I noticed that the controller plugged in was a joystick. When you played 'Indy 500,' you needed a special paddle controller to play it, so I knew something strange was going on, and I got a bad case of the "hee-bee gee-bees." It's the first time I can remember the feeling of being watched, and I looked around the room cautiously with a heightened sense of awareness. It's a strange feeling you get when you've been pulled into the world of unexplainable and paranormal. I knew with one hundred percent certainty that I did not put that cartridge in the console, so the question was now – who did? I didn't tell my sister because I knew that I would be leaving soon, and she'd be alone knowing this information. It was bad enough that the vacuum turned on by itself; I didn't want to make things worse. I'm almost positive that my deceased father was responsible for the cartridge switch. As I mentioned earlier in the book, my dad only played one Atari game, and that game was 'Indy 500.' I think it was his way of saying hello, but I kept thinking, "How is this possible?" How could a ghost do that? From that point going forward, I had a different perspective on the world.

Changing more than clothes

Back when I worked at Bradlees department store, I was working in the dressing rooms to make sure nobody stole any clothes, etc. There were three changing rooms, marked 1, 2, and 3. There was someone down the end at #3, no one in #1, and this middle-aged woman went into #2. After about ten minutes, the girl in #3 left, which left only the woman, still in #2. A few minutes later, a woman leaves the middle dressing room, but it wasn't the same woman who went in! She had on similar clothes, but it was a younger woman and clearly not the same person. As she walked out, she smiled at me, but there was an underlying creepiness about her gaze. I checked all three rooms and they were empty. I know what I saw, and I'm telling you, it was a different woman.

Bobo the cat (and now the dog)

A couple of years after I moved out of my sister Cassie's house, I stopped by to say hi to everyone. I noticed that they had a black cat now, which was about six months old. It was very cute, and I asked my niece Leann, "What's the cat's name?" She said, "BoBo." Now, mind you, I told my sister and her husband very little about the events that took place while using the Ouija board over there, and I know that I definitely did not tell them BoBo's name or any other name. I didn't talk a lot about it because I didn't want to freak out with my sister, and then she told me to stop using the board in her house, so I kept most everything to myself. When I heard the cat's name was BoBo, I had a very disturbing feeling. At that point, I felt almost obligated to tell them about BoBo, but once I did, they didn't believe me. I had no proof or verification. My friend Garett, who used to use the board with me, was currently incarcerated, so they couldn't appreciate the correlation of it all. Of all the names in the world you could give to a pet, they chose BOBO! I mean, c'mon!

Update

As I'm writing this book, I asked my brother-in-law Jesse about some of the details of his story, which I included. He and his friend Deb love Yorkshire Terriers and have one of their own. An elderly woman in Peabody needed to get rid of her "yorkie" and didn't want to give it to a shelter due to the possibility of euthanasia, so Jesse and Deb "saved" it. They asked the woman the dog's name, and she said "BoBo." Jesse confirmed that it was spelled as B O B O. They immediately changed it to "Beau." I had to add this to the book because WOW! This is way beyond being a coincidence. Creepy.

The sneaker

In the Summer of 2002, I was visiting my sister Judy up in New Hampshire for the weekend. One of my favorite things to do up there was to take the canoe all around the pond where she lived. The water's edge was no more than fifty feet from the house, so you could get on the canoe and just go. During this particular trip, I ventured off down to the other side of the pond and inside this small, quiet cove. Nobody resided there, so it was eerily quiet and overgrown with vines, ornamental grass, and shrubbery. The scrub brush formed an archway at the entrance, so upon entering, you could tell that nature had taken hold of this section of the pond. It was overrun with bullfrogs, insects, and other wildlife. The cove was about one hundred feet in diameter, and as I approached the middle, I noticed a large fallen limb with something white attached to it. The closer I got, I noticed that the white object was a basketball sneaker. The company's name on it was 'Avia,' it was mostly white, and what looked like blue on the back of it. It was waterlogged, faded from the sun, and the leather was cracked. I didn't touch it because it had all kinds of nasty stuff on it, like mud, algae, and God knows what else inside of it. When I got back to my sister's, I told her about the sneaker, and she told me that about five years prior, one of her neighbors' teenage sons had committed suicide by drowning himself in the pond. I asked, "This pond?" My sister replied, "Yes." I asked her if she thought the sneaker belonged to that kid, and my sister said that she wasn't sure. A couple of weeks later, my sister called me to let me know that the sneaker did, in fact, belong to her neighbor Caroline's son. When I heard this news, I felt very sad that someone so young would take their life in such a horrific way. I also got the willies because I saw his shoe, and most likely the last place this kid was alive, unless the current took it over there. To think that of all the times I swam in that pond, there were the remains of a person at the bottom. I don't want to sound insensitive, but when I heard of this news, the first thing I thought of was the ending scene in the original 'Friday the 13th' movie, when the young version of Jason jumps out of the water and attacks the woman in a canoe! I can only wonder what else lies at the bottom of that pond.

De Ja Vu, or something else

The following year, in the Summer of 2003, I was heading into a Walmart, and as I was entering, I saw this guy leaving. There were about eight or so people between him and me. This guy looked extremely familiar to me, and I kept thinking, "Where do I know this guy from??" He was as familiar to me as, let's say, my mailman or an employee at my local coffee shop. I just couldn't place him, and his identity escaped me completely. He gave me a head nod as if to say, "Hey man, what's up?" while smiling, but I couldn't reciprocate the gesture because, for the life of me, I didn't know who he was. I was embarrassed by my ignorance of not knowing him, and as I turned into the store, he stopped smiling because he probably thought I was blowing him off, and he looked bummed out as a result. I should have known this guy, but I didn't. He looked so familiar, but I couldn't place him, and it was driving me bonkers. Usually, if I can't remember something like the name of a movie or an actor or a song lyric for a couple of days, it'll pop into my head, but this guy's identity has escaped me for about twenty years now! I try every now and then to figure it out, but to no avail, so I basically gave up on trying to figure out who he was. It's not like this guy mistakenly took me for someone else, because he looked familiar to me as well. Maybe I knew this guy in another life or dimension. Maybe one of us had an alternate reality, or both. I know that I knew this guy from somewhere; I have a sixth sense for that sort of thing. Maybe he didn't belong, or maybe I didn't belong. It seemed to be a glitch in the matrix, and I truly believe in a higher power that can randomly pluck us out of a certain existence and place us in another one, to either help us and guide us or to teach us something for spiritual growth. I also believe that this transition is detected or not detected based on the recipient's need for awareness, with divine intervention or a seamless transition with no knowledge of any such change.

Good Samaritan from nowhere

My cousin Erica was driving in Wakefield, zipping along during a busy time of the day, when the traffic was congested. Sure enough, she got into a fender bender. I guess the guy in front of her slammed on his brakes, and the person behind her slammed into her, causing Erica to get whiplash. Within minutes, the police, fire department, and EMTs showed up, and they told her not to move. Out of the corner of her eye, she saw a middle-aged man dressed in what looked like 1940s attire with a fedora and all. He walked in front of the car without looking in and then opened the rear door and sat right behind Erica. Strangely, she wasn't scared as the man put his hands around her neck and whispered to her, "You're gonna be alright." The outside commotion was oblivious to what was going on inside Erica's car. Suddenly, the man exited the vehicle, and she noticed that the pain in her neck was gone. Then one of the EMT guys told her to be calm, as they're going to get a gurney for her. Erica told him that she didn't need one because that guy helped her, and she asked him, "Did you see where he went?" The EMT guy said, "Who?" Then she explained to him all about this man who helped her with her neck, and that he was wearing out-of-date clothing. The paramedics put Erica on the gurney and brought her to the hospital. The x-rays showed no damage to her neck or spinal cord, so she was released. When Erica told me this story, I asked her what this guy's face looked like. She told me that she really didn't see his face because of the way he walked, and when he got in the car, she couldn't move her head, and the rear-view mirror got damaged from the accident. Once he fixed my neck, he was just gone, and nobody else saw him. She said during the whole encounter, from the moment I saw this guy, I was calm and at ease. I think that this good Samaritan was most likely a ghost or spirit of some kind, firstly, because of his clothes, and also because he walked amongst a pretty big accident scene with dozens of first responders moving about while going completely undetected.

UFO

What book of paranormal short stories would be complete without a good old-fashioned UFO encounter included within its pages? In the summer of 1970, in Salem, Massachusetts, my sister Deborrah and her husband Jesse were enjoying the night air near the water's edge at a place called Salem Willows Park. It's a place I've been to many times myself, and it's a great place to bring the whole family with its many ice cream stands and arcades. It's also a romantic spot for a young couple to take a stroll, holding hands, while walking near the harbor, enjoying the view of the many boats docked for the evening. It was a clear night, perfect for stargazing. The two of them walked away from the bright lights and noisy activity, found themselves near the tree line about one hundred yards from the crowd. Suddenly, they noticed coming from their left over the trees about one hundred feet in the air, a silver-colored disc-shaped saucer with multi-colored lights blinking around the middle of it. My sister told me it was about thirty feet in diameter and made absolutely no sound whatsoever. Deborrah passed away in 2019, and I never knew her to lie. So, when she told me this story around 1985 or so, I took it for gospel. I've also talked to my brother-in-law Jesse about the encounter, and his version was the same as my sister's. Jesse is a man of integrity, so I knew this story was legit. I had a UFO encounter of my own, but not nearly as impressive as my sister's. I was camping in the White Mountains of New Hampshire some years back with some friends. As I was looking up at the stars, I noticed about ten or so little specs of light in a line formation going from left to right. From the time I noticed them until they were out of sight on the right side of the observable night sky, only about five seconds had elapsed. I could tell these specs of light were extremely high up. Based on that, these objects were moving at about 100,000 mph! I've seen the ISS move along the night sky, and it appears to be moving more slowly by comparison, even though it's traveling at about 17,000 mph. The ISS is about 250 miles up, and these specs seemed to be at roughly the same height, and they moved at least twenty times faster than the ISS. The buddies I was with thought they were satellites, and I explained to them that satellites don't travel in a formation like that, number one. Number two, they certainly do not travel at that speed. Based on the number of beers consumed by them at that point, my explanation had fallen on deaf (drunk) ears.

The phone call

My sister Deborrah told me this story about twenty-five years ago, around 2005, and I never forgot it because it's just so creepy and amazing. Her mother-in-law, Esther, passed away in 1972. The day after her passing, my sister was in her kitchen having tea, and on the wall next to her was a clock with a loud tick that suddenly stopped ticking. My sister said she felt like she was being watched, then the kitchen phone rang, making her jump. She nervously picked up the receiver and said hello. To her astonishment, it was her recently deceased mother-in-law, Esther, on the other end. She told my sister that she loved her and that everything was going to be okay. As I said before, my sister Deborrah was very honest, so I believe this story to be true. I'm amazed that a spirit on the other side would be able to communicate and interact with a living person by using a telephone. I'd love to hear a scientist's opinion on how they think my sister got a phone call from her deceased mother-in-law, because I know it really happened. When I try to make sense of it, I can't wrap my head around it.

Crystal clear message

My brother-in-law Jess's sister Crystal passed away in 2000, and about a year later, he was going out to his car and saw his sister Crystal sitting in the driver's seat. Jesse told me that the really strange part of it all, besides the fact that his deceased sister was in his car, was that her eyes had what looked like white clouds in them! He ran inside to get his friend Deb, and when she saw Crystal in the car, she screamed and fell down, practically fainting. They went back inside, and Deb had to compose herself. About ten minutes later, they went back outside to see if she was still there, but she was gone. A short time later, Jesse, who worked in a metal fabrication shop, removed a factory-installed plastic strap from a stack of sheet metal to be fed into a machine to form certain parts for various vendors. The strapping was the kind you'd see to hold a pallet of bricks together or to prevent a bundle of lumber from shifting during shipping. So, this stack of sheet metal hadn't been tampered with by anyone in that area and certainly not by anyone in his shop. It most likely came from halfway across the country, yet as Jesse fed through the sheet metal piece by piece, he noticed one of the pieces of metal halfway down the stack had some writing on it. The writing said, "Love you, Jessa." Jessa was the nickname his sister Crystal gave him. How is it possible for a message to be inscribed on a piece of sheet metal, in the middle of the stack, from a remote location, knowing that her brother would see it? I've never known anyone in my life to be named Jessa, except for my brother-in-law Jesse, so it was not a coincidence. It was undeniable proof that his sister Crystal put that there for him to see. There's no logical explanation for it, but as impossible as it may seem, it really happened.

Strange scream

Back in 2017, I was apartment searching in New Hampshire near the White Mountains. I didn't realize the area was so far north. I just got in my truck and away I went. By the time I got there, it was dark and very foggy, so the visibility was horrible. I never got the apartment, thank God, because of the distance, but on the way back to my truck, I heard the scariest scream/roar I ever heard. I could tell it was straight ahead from where I was, on top of the mountain I was at the base of. From the distance it came from, I could tell it was extremely loud. I know this is going to sound weird, but it sounded like a giant woman with a respiratory problem, screaming for help. They were long, drawn-out screams/roars, suggesting that this creature was large enough to be able to scream that loud for that long. I say creature because I know it wasn't a bear because bears growl deeper and not nearly as long. It wasn't a bobcat or cougar because they roar with a higher pitch and not for long. I ruled out Elk or Moose because they have a honking sound, and again, for a short duration. This scream sounded very human, but big, and it had a whiny guttural scream mixed with a deep growl. I'm a pretty big guy and can scream loudly when I have to, but there's no way I would have been heard from the distance this thing was at, and definitely not nearly for as long. Whatever this thing was, it was big and it was really upset. So, I got in my truck and high-tailed it out of there.

Baby powder

Around December 2021, my wife and I were dressing our infant daughter Kate, and I was on diaper detail. I put a little powder on her before I put a new diaper on. I noticed she needed a little bit more powder, so I went to reach for it, which was just on my left, and the powder wasn't there. I thought it fell off the bed where I was changing her, but it wasn't on the floor either. I told my wife, Oksana, to watch our daughter while I looked for it. It was one of those little travel-sized bottles, so I figured it fell between the mattress and the frame – nothing. Oksana put Kate in her bassinet, and then we both looked. She knew that I had the powder right there, and she saw me using it. So, then we scoured the whole bedroom, and still we found nothing! Last year, in 2024, we rearranged the bedroom and took everything out, and even took the bed frame apart, and no baby powder! It just vanished into thin air. It was right next to me one minute, and then it disappeared. It would be no different if you were eating dinner, with your plate in front of you and your drink off to the side, and all of a sudden, your drink disappears!

Ida

The following year, in 2022, I saw this medium on the internet, and he was supposed to be really good at contacting spirits that have moved on. So, I paid a small fee to join in on one of his Zoom sessions that had about twenty people on it. The session I was in was for ninety minutes, and each person's turn took about twenty minutes on average. So, I figured that if I got a turn, it would be luck of the draw. After ninety minutes had expired, I was no longer able to interact with the group. I guess others paid more than me because they were still on the Zoom call. I could listen to it, but I couldn't be heard. Right before I was going to leave the session, the medium said, "I have an Ida coming through, does anyone know an Ida?" I said to my wife, who was sitting right next to me, "My grandmother's name was Ida; it was my mother's mother." I told my wife that I was expecting either my mother or my father to come through. I never met any of my grandparents, so why would they be reaching out to me instead of my parents? It had to have been my grandmother because Ida is an extremely rare name, but it worried me a little because I feared that they were disappointed with me or something. I was really hoping to talk to them to find out if they are proud of me. I plan on visiting a psychic in the near future, and hopefully, I will get some positive feedback.

Pen cap

This happened after I wrote this book. I was discussing a to-do list with my wife, and I had a pen in one hand and the cap in the other. As I was talking to her, I was fidgeting with the cap, and then I put it on the kitchen table to my left. After about ten minutes of talking, I went to put the cap back on the pen. I'm very neurotic about pen caps and the fear of a given pen or marker drying out. So, I'm looking for the cap and I can't find it. I told Oksana, and she said, "No way!" This was just like the baby powder incident. I had that cap minutes before, and then, like the powder, it was gone.

Hello?

This, like the pen cap incident, happened after I finished this book, but I had to include it. I'm a bit of a night owl, so the other night, I was in the bathroom at the sink getting ready to shave. I didn't have the water on yet, so it was very quiet in the house, and that's exactly why I stay up late. I heard my wife getting out of bed, which was in the next room over, and she approached the door. I was waiting for her to knock like she always does, but she didn't. I was going to say "honey?" but I stared at the bottom of the door for about five seconds, and then she turned around and went towards the living room instead of back to our bedroom. I figured she changed her mind or something, but I found it weird that she didn't say anything. I opened the door and looked in the living room, and there was nobody there. I checked the boys' rooms and they were sound asleep. Then I checked my bedroom, and Oksana and Kate were sound asleep also. So, the question is, who was standing on the other side of the bathroom door?

Summary

I have many regrets from engaging with the occult and various paranormal entities I've encountered over half of my life. It has opened my eyes, however, to what exists in other realms and planes of existence. I don't know exactly who I contacted during my many accounts, but I know they were highly intelligent, because the demons know everything about you. They're very powerful, manipulative, and from what I've heard from various sources, have a great hatred towards us humans. I found BoBo to be very deceptive, and towards the end of my Ouija board usage, he wanted me to do bad things to people, which I never intended from the beginning. I was a broken man who had just lost both his parents, and as a result, had a huge disdain towards life, and I believe BoBo fed off that. Their death left a huge hole in my heart, and I was trying to fill it anyway I could. I unfortunately went down the wrong path, following Satan's lead. I've done a lot of bad things in my life, and these days I'm trying to score points with God by praying daily for forgiveness. I don't recommend anyone who has lost their way to start using a Ouija board or tarot cards for any reason. If you're trying to communicate with a loved one, I suggest praying to them, and at some point, you'll get a response. By dabbling with the occult, you're opening doors for demonic entities to enter your world, and that is not a good thing! In my opinion, I don't think Ouija boards should be sold as a board game and should not be so easily available. An Ouija board is not a game and shouldn't be treated as such. It's been twelve years since I dabbled with the occult, and I'm sure that BoBo lingers around me waiting for me to try to communicate with him, but that will never happen again. Maybe he's trying to communicate with me, but I'm not open for business anymore. I'm truly convinced that my mother is my guardian angel and that she protects me and watches over me. When I'm depressed or having a tough time with something, I feel her presence. I heard that when you die, you're greeted by demons in disguise as humans. They lead you to a completely dark void if you've not let Jesus into your life and sinned without regret. The demons then show their real, grotesque, and somewhat reptilian appearance, as they torment and torture you for all of eternity. You must call out to Jesus and ask for forgiveness, and if Jesus thinks you deserve one more chance of redemption, the love that Jesus has for you will save you. If I could do things over again, I wouldn't go near a Ouija board, but I fear that I've burned all my bridges with the lord and I will suffer an eternal living death by the very same demons that guided me to sin in the first place. I fear that when my physical body dies, I will be transported through a "blacker than black" portal and get slammed to the fiery ground of Hell, and as I look up, I'll be facing the real BoBo himself.

www.ingramcontent.com/pod-product-compliance
Lightning Source LLC
Chambersburg PA
CBHW070205100426
42743CB00013B/3059